Because Writing Matters

Because Writing Matters

IMPROVING STUDENT WRITING IN OUR SCHOOLS

National Writing Project

and Carl Nagin

JOSSEY-BASS
A Wiley Imprint
www.josseybass.com

24.95

Published by Jossey-Bass
A Wiley Imprint
989 Market Street, San Francisco, CA 94103-1741   www.josseybass.com

Jossey-Bass books and products are available through most bookstores. To contact Jossey-Bass directly call our Customer Care Department within the U.S. at 800-956-7739, outside the U.S. at 317-572-3986, or fax 317-572-4002.

Jossey-Bass also publishes its books in a variety of electronic formats. Some content that appears in print may not be available in electronic books.

Library of Congress Cataloging-in-Publication Data

National Writing Project (U.S.)
   Because writing matters : improving student writing in our schools /
National Writing Project and Carl Nagin.—1st ed.
      p. cm. — (The Jossey-Bass education series)
Includes bibliographical references (p.   ) and index.
   ISBN 0-7879-6562-6 (alk. paper)
   1. English language—Composition and exercises—Study and
teaching—United States. I. Nagin, Carl, 1946– II. Title. III. Series.
   PE1405.U6N38 2003
                                                           2002155027

Printed in the United States of America
FIRST EDITION
HB Printing   10 9 8 7 6 5

The Jossey-Bass Education Series

CONTENTS

PREFACE

For nearly three decades, the core mission of the National Writing Project (NWP) has been to improve writing and learning in our schools by improving the teaching of writing. Through a teachers-teaching-teachers professional development model, the NWP disseminates the exemplary classroom practices of successful teachers to teachers in all disciplines and at all grade levels. Apart from the NWP's direct experience in working with teachers in every state, the past three decades have also yielded a rich vein of new research about writing—how it is learned, practiced, and assessed; its impact on how children learn to read; and the sociocultural factors that influence its development. Yet surprisingly little of these new data and understanding—some of which originated with the NWP—have reached the general public; nor do these new findings inform much current debate about educational reform. The challenge has been to gather and disseminate this knowledge to decision makers who may lack the time to sort through this diverse and complex body of educational research and hands-on experience. How does it all translate into an action plan, and how does it fit into a curriculum that must be assessed and achieve results?

The idea for a book that examines the condition of writing in our nation's schools has developed as the National Writing Project has worked with administrators and policymakers in advancing its core mission. Local writing project site leaders have seen the need for such a work—one that would draw on what the NWP has learned about teaching writing and make that knowledge available to a broad audience, including policymakers, school administrators, teachers, parents, and others concerned with education reform. Among the many books about writing, none, NWP directors have observed, synthesizes current research and presents the case for teaching writing well in a way that is persuasive to decision makers, administrators, and the general public.

Such a book is no small order. Writing, as many educators have noted recently, remains the "silent R" in the traditional triad of what students need to learn. Today, there is an urgency to reconsider the relationship of writing to learning as well as the place of writing in our schools as we make every effort to meet our students' needs in the information age and prepare them to become informed and active citizens in the twenty-first century.

To examine how the teaching of writing can be improved and to present what is known about effective programs and practices, the National Writing Project asked Carl Nagin, an award-winning journalist and teacher of writing, to research and write this book. As part of that effort, Nagin conducted extensive interviews with principals, district superintendents, teachers, and education researchers to identify the core challenges and issues these educators face in building effective writing programs. The book offers case studies of how teachers and administrators have worked together to meet those challenges, both in individual classrooms and as part of a sustained, schoolwide effort. *Because Writing Matters* shows how research-based strategies have been developed into successful practice and programs. It makes the case for the importance of writing for those who recognize the need to improve it and seek models for reaching that goal.

Richard Sterling
Executive Director
National Writing Project

The National Writing Project (NWP) is a professional development network dedicated to improving student writing and
learning by improving the teaching of writing in U.S. schools.
Begun in 1973 at the University of California, Berkeley, the NWP
is a steadily growing network of more than 175 sites in 50 states,
Washington, D.C., Puerto Rico, and the U.S. Virgin Islands. NWP
sites use a teachers-teaching-teachers model that draws on the
knowledge, expertise, and leadership of successful classroom
teachers to annually serve more than 100,000 teachers, grades
K–16, in all disciplines. Numerous research studies demonstrate
the success of the NWP model in improving student writing
achievement. Support for the National Writing Project is provided by the U.S. Department of Education, foundations, cor-
porations, universities, and K–12 schools.

Carl Nagin is a journalist, editor, and teacher. He has worked
for the PBS series *Frontline,* and his articles have appeared in
such national publications as the *New Yorker,* the *New York
Times,* and *Art & Antiques.* A four-time recipient of grants from

the National Endowment for the Humanities, Nagin has received awards for his teaching, research, and documentary films. He taught writing at high school and college levels for more than fifteen years as a faculty member at Harvard University and at the New England Conservatory of Music, where he directed the freshman writing program. As an editor, he has worked on K–12 curriculum projects for the Massachusetts Department of Education and for the Developmental Studies Center in Oakland, California. Nagin currently resides in Berkeley, California.

The Authors

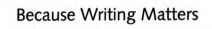Because Writing Matters

INTRODUCTION
Why Writing Matters

Concern with the quality of student writing has been a perennial feature of the American educational landscape. What has changed are assumptions about its uses and importance both within and outside the classroom as well as what educators have learned about teaching it. The need for freshman writing courses, one of the most consistently required subjects in the postsecondary curriculum, dates back to 1874, when Harvard University began requiring a written entrance exam. Harvard's version of the course came in response to the poor writing of its upperclassmen[1] and the results of its entrance exam, which more than half the candidates—"products of America's best preparatory schools—failed."[2]

For most of the nineteenth century, according to Arthur Applebee, director of the National Research Center on English Language Achievement (CELA), "the teaching of writing [in elementary and secondary schools] focused on penmanship and little else. Later, writing instruction was often postponed until the middle and upper grades," on the notion that students first had to achieve basic literacy in reading.[3] Writing was something of a silent "R," even among Progressives, whose influence on writing pedagogy was "limited to writing about personal experiences or about experiential connections to literature."[4]

A little more than a century after Harvard instituted its written entrance exam, a 1975 *Newsweek* article ("Why Johnny Can't Write")[5] proclaimed that America had a writing crisis, only this time the onus was placed on *public* schools for neglecting "the basics." Clearly, this was not a new controversy. What was changing was how educators and policymakers were defining our literacy needs, which in turn changed expectations for writing curricula in terms of their scope and context. The controversy fueled a boom in university-level remedial courses and programs to address the deficient literacy skills of entering freshmen. It also led to creation of the National Writing Project (NWP), whose mission and professional development model are committed to bringing exemplary writing instruction to all of America's schools. Despite repeated "back-to-basics" efforts, the need for improving student writing persists. It raises the question, Why is writing so challenging to teach and learn?

UCLA's Mike Rose suggests that the stakes for learning to write have changed. The benchmark for what counts as literate writing, what good writing requires, and how many people need to be literate in our society has moved dramatically since the nineteenth century. It is no longer the concern, as it was at Harvard in 1874, of an exclusively white, male elite; in today's increasingly diverse society, writing is a gateway for success in academia, the new workplace, and the global economy, as well as for our collective success as a participatory democracy. The good news is that our understanding of how to teach writing has evolved significantly over the last three decades. Successful strategies as well

> Many young people come to university able to summarize the events in a news story or write a personal response to a play. . . . But they have considerable trouble with what has come to be called critical literacy: framing an argument or taking someone else's argument apart [and] synthesizing different points of view. . . . The authors of the [writing] crisis reports got tremendously distressed about students' difficulties with such tasks, but it's important to remember that, traditionally, such abilities have only been developed in an elite: in priests, scholars, or a leisure class. Ours is the first society in history to expect so many of its people to be able to perform these very sophisticated literacy activities.
>
> Mike Rose,
> *Lives on the Boundary*, p. 188

as models and resources for building an effective writing program in a school are known and available. So today, the need to improve writing is perhaps better framed as a challenge rather than a crisis.

Because Writing Matters describes the current state of teaching writing in America, highlighting effective classroom practices and successful school programs. The National Writing Project conceived of this book as a resource for school administrators, educators, and policymakers who want to know how to address the challenge of improving student writing at all grade levels. Its purpose is threefold:

1. To make the case that writing is a complex activity; more than just a skill or talent, it is a means of inquiry and expression for learning in all grades and disciplines

2. To examine current trends, best practices, research, and issues in the teaching of writing, such as its role in early literacy; how the process of the writer in the real world can be developed in the classroom; how writing can be fairly and authentically assessed; and how writing can be taught across the curriculum

3. To offer practical solutions and models for school administrators and policymakers involved in planning, implementing, and assessing a writing program as well as those seeking effective staff development for teaching writing

Effective writing skills are important in all stages of life from early education to future employment. In the business world, as well as in school, students must convey complex ideas and information in a clear, succinct manner. Inadequate writing skills, therefore, could inhibit achievement across the curriculum and in future careers, while proficient writing skills help students convey ideas, deliver instructions, analyze information, and motivate others.

National Center for Education Statistics, U.S. Department of Education, *The Condition of Education*, p. 70

This book takes a pragmatic approach to the challenge of improving writing and building successful programs in our schools. Through vignettes and case studies, it illustrates how educators have used writing in diverse classroom and school settings to enrich learning and provide meaningful learning experiences for students at all grade levels. It addresses these core questions:

- Why does writing matter?
- What does research say about the teaching of writing?
- What do we mean by "writing processes"?
- What are some features of an effective writing classroom?
- How can writing be used to develop critical thinking?
- How does writing fit into learning across disciplines?
- What kind of professional development prepares teachers to teach and use writing?
- What does a schoolwide writing program look like?
- What are fair ways to assess writing?

The book draws from a persuasive body of research over the past three decades that is changing how writing is taught in many classrooms and our understanding of how it can affect learning. The research has brought the practice of writers in the real world into the classroom. It has added new insights about how writing and reading are linked in early literacy. For our increasingly diverse classrooms, it has also illuminated many of the social and cultural factors that support literacy development. In addition, this book draws from interviews with teachers, principals, and superintendents who have taken on the challenge of building a successful writing program in their school, classroom, or district—educators working in diverse settings across the country. Some (but not all) of them are associated with the NWP.

For more than a quarter century, the NWP has made improving the quality of writing and learning in our nation's schools its central mission. What began in the summer of 1974 as a professional development institute for twenty-five teachers on the University of California campus in Berkeley has evolved into a network of 175 NWP sites in fifty states, Washington, D.C., Puerto Rico, and the U.S. Virgin Islands, involving more than two million teachers at urban, rural, and suburban schools in realizing its core goal. In 2000–01, these sites led more than three thousand in-service workshops for teachers, with more than a third of these programs as part of ongoing partnerships with schools. Serving more than 125,000 educators a year in all disciplines in grades K–16 (roughly one out of forty teachers in the United States), it is the only national program that focuses on writing as a means to improve learning in America's schools.

The book draws from a persuasive body of research over the past three decades that is changing how writing is taught in many classrooms and our understanding of how it can affect learning.

Since its inception, the NWP has fostered university-school collaboration. From that collective effort, much has been learned about exemplary teaching practices in writing and their impact on students' learning throughout their academic careers. This knowledge has been broadened by research over the last three decades in the field of composition pedagogy, leading to new understanding about the role of writing in our classrooms that has critical implications for educational reform efforts. Policymakers and school administrators, no less than teachers and parents, can benefit from understanding current trends and issues in the teaching of writing and the vital role it can play in achieving quality and excellence in our classrooms across the disciplines.

Today, more and more educators have come to understand that writing is central to academic success. Although successful teaching strategies have been identified and innovative programs implemented with a demonstrable impact on student learning, their broad dissemination remains a critical challenge for serious school reform. Paradoxically (with the exception of college-level teaching geared to the freshman writer), composition pedagogy remains a neglected area of study at most of the nation's thirteen hundred schools of education, where future public school teachers are trained. Nor is it a specific requirement in most state teacher certification programs. To some extent, the place of writing in educational reform, and debate over its role in developing literacy, has been overshadowed or subsumed by the controversy surrounding the reading wars.

Because Writing Matters makes the case that students need to write *more* across all content areas and that schools need to expand their writing curricula to involve students in a range of writing tasks. The challenge has been echoed at the national level by the National Assessment of Educational Progress (NAEP), the National Council of Teachers of English (NCTE), the American Association of School Administrators (AASA), and the National Academy of Education's Commission on Reading: "Unfortunately, every recent analysis of writing instruction in American classrooms has reached the same conclusion: Children don't get many opportunities to write. In one recent study in grades one, three, and five, only 15 percent of the school day was spent in any kind of writing activity. Two-thirds of the writing that did occur was word-for-word copying in workbooks. Compositions of a paragraph or more in length are infrequent even at the high school level."[6]

> Because Writing Matters *makes the case that students need to write* more *across all content areas and that schools need to expand their writing curricula to involve students in a range of writing tasks.*

Because Writing Matters examines what school administrators can do to meet the writing challenge in our nation's schools. It explores the research-based teaching strategies that can improve writing and presents case studies of how effective, schoolwide writing programs have been designed in a variety of school settings.

Chapter One explores why writing is complex and what challenges a school must meet to teach it well. It argues that although everyone can and should learn to write, teaching writing well remains one of the key tasks facing schools today as they work to meet increasingly high standards and expectations for learning.

Chapter Two summarizes relevant research from the past three decades about how writers compose and develop. It explores how social and cognitive perspectives on writing have transformed our understanding of how writing can be used in the classroom. It examines the links between writing and reading in early literacy and why many researchers believe that writing instruction must begin in the earliest grades.

Chapter Three presents evidence from national assessments about what improves student writing. What are the most promising strategies and classroom practices? Can writing support learning in a content-heavy area such as science or math? It explores how writing across the curriculum can be used to support a high level of learning and the need to incorporate critical thinking and inquiry strategies in writing tasks.

Chapter Four makes the case for professional development in teaching writing and why it is a crucial element of school reform. It also describes the history and rationale for the NWP model of professional development: teachers teaching teachers.

In Chapter Five, the thorny challenge posed by state standards and assessments for writing is examined. The chapter suggests some ABCs of writing assessment and how it can best be used to understand student progress and development. What is a fair rubric for assessing writing, and what are some effective assessment models? It also examines what a recent study of mandatory state writing assessments has shown about their impact on teaching.

Finally, Chapter Six explores the role of principals and superintendents in helping to build an effective writing program. It presents case studies of how two schools, urban and suburban, developed successful schoolwide writing programs, what challenges they faced, and the results they have achieved.

Models of effective teaching practice, schoolwide writing programs, and the research supporting them have a new urgency for educators, policymakers, and parents today. Each year, nearly 1.3 million high school seniors take the SAT, the most widely used college-entrance exam. As this book went to press, the College Board announced that, beginning in spring 2005, it will require students to complete a 50- to 60-minute writing test as part of its revised SAT I exam. The new essay component, according to the *New York*

Times, has already received broad support in colleges and universities. "I think it will lead to real reform," says William Fitzsimmons, dean of admissions at Harvard University, "particularly in high schools that haven't been doing a good job in teaching writing."[7]

Although questions have been raised as to the quality and fairness of the proposed exam, it reflects a significant shift in educators' thinking about writing as a tool for student success in college and beyond. University of California president Richard C. Atkinson hails it as "a transforming event in the nature of education," noting, "It sends a message to all students that they need to start writing early in their career."[8]

Because Writing Matters presents a vision of how our schools can help students meet that need.

Improving Student Writing
Challenges and Expectations

Writing is complex, and so is the instruction that a school must provide if its students are to reach the high standards of learning expected of them. Even the most accomplished writers say that writing is challenging, most notably because there is so much uncertainty embedded in the process of doing it. The writer doesn't always know beforehand where to begin, much less how to proceed. Writing doesn't take shape all at once in fluent sentences and organized paragraphs. The more complex the subject or task, the more disorderly and unpredictable the journey can be. Not even experienced writers "get it right" the first time through. Most would agree with *New Yorker* writer E. B. White when he said that "the best writing is rewriting." Writing is hard because it is a struggle of thought, feeling, and imagination to find expression clear enough for the task at hand.

Doing it well means being both a writer and a reader. As writer, we look *through* language and struggle to discover what we mean to say; as reader (of our own work), we look *at* language with an editor's eye to be sure we've found the right words to say what we mean. "Read and revise, reread and revise," counsels literary critic Jacques Barzun; "keep reading and revising until your text seems adequate to your thought." Sometimes, the professionals tell us, this means letting yourself write poorly at the start, with the expectation of improving it further down the line. "You have to get the bulk of it done," says writer Larry Gelbart, "and then you start to refine it. You have to put down less-than-marvelous material just to keep going, whatever you think the end is going to be—which may be something else altogether by the time you get there."[1]

White, Barzun, and Gelbart are variously describing what researchers call the recursive nature of writing. Studies of how writers actually work show them shuffling through phases of planning, reflection, drafting, and revision, though rarely in a linear fashion. Each phase requires problem solving and critical thinking. More than adequacy of expression per se is required. Successful writers grasp the occasion, purpose, and audience for their work. They have learned how to juggle the expectations of diverse readers and the demands of distinct forms. Writing a letter or a persuasive editorial is not the same as fashioning a moving poem or a tightly reasoned legal brief.

Studies of how writers actually work show them shuffling through phases of planning, reflection, drafting, and revision, though rarely in a linear fashion. Each phase requires problem solving and critical thinking.

If writing is challenging, teaching it is all the more so. How do we create a classroom or school where increasingly complex writing tasks can be learned by all students? Teacher and researcher James Moffett described the new consensus about effective composition pedagogy this way: "Writing has to be learned in school very much the same way that it is practiced out of school. This means that the writer has a reason to write, an intended audience, and control of subject and form. It also means that composing is staged across various phases of rumination, investigation, consultation with others, drafting, feedback, revision, and perfecting."[2]

This understanding poses new challenges for educators as to how writing is presented and practiced in the classroom. Many of us can recall an English essay returned to us with marginal comments such as "This needs to be clearer" or "Weak opening" or "This paragraph is hard to follow." Often, no instruction or roadmap accompanied the comment showing how to take the next step. As students, we were just expected to fix these things and get them right the next time, as if writing well required the same kind of knowledge as making a subject and verb agree or spelling a word correctly. But how *do* we make writing clear? Does everyone agree on what a strong opening looks like? What should we do to make our sentences flow in paragraphs that are easy to follow? If only these results *could* be drilled into us, then teaching writing would be easy.

Challenging as it is, educators interviewed for this publication argued that all students can learn to write and that writing is the most visible expression not only of what their students know but also of how well they have learned it. Those interviewed were teachers from all grade levels, elementary to postsecondary; language arts coordinators; composition program directors; principals; and superintendents. They underscored the critical role writing can play as a means for learning in most academic subjects. Some characterized writing as the most important academic skill students need to develop in their secondary and postsecondary education. All of them cited the hurdles schools and educators face in meeting students' writing needs.

Educators interviewed for this publication
argued that all students can learn to write
and that writing is the most visible expression
not only of what their students know
but also of how well they have learned it.

This chapter examines why improving writing is sometimes so challenging, for teacher and student alike. It identifies and explores some of the complexity that educators and policymakers should understand if they are to develop and sustain an effective writing program or curriculum. It addresses as well some of the myths and realities surrounding the teaching and learning of writing and suggests how administrators can assess how well writing is being taught in their schools.

HOW EDUCATORS SEE THE CHALLENGES OF TEACHING AND LEARNING WRITING

What does a school need to provide if its students are to master the complex set of skills and knowledge called writing? Educators interviewed for this book described two kinds of challenges for improving the quality of writing in a school. The first addresses what students need in order to develop and improve as writers. The second reflects how teachers and administrators must support and sustain effective writing instruction.

Students Need to Write More in All Subjects

Learning to write requires frequent, supportive practice. Evidence shows that writing performance improves when a student writes often and across content areas. Writing also affects reading comprehension. According to a 1998 National Assessment of Educational Progress (NAEP) reading report card,[3] students in grades four, eight, and twelve who said they wrote long answers on a weekly basis scored higher than those who said they never or hardly ever did so. (The NAEP reports are discussed in more detail in Chapter Three.)

> *Learning to write requires frequent, supportive practice.*

Yet many American schools are not giving students much time to write. Sixty-nine percent of fourth grade teachers report spending ninety minutes or less per week on writing activities, according to data collected for the

NAEP 1998 Writing Assessment. Many of these activities require only a brief response rather than the longer ones NAEP assesses. National studies and assessments of writing over the past three decades have repeatedly shown that students spend too little time writing in and out of school. When a school focuses on improving writing, it often starts with a realistic assessment of how much and what kind of writing students are actually asked to do.

Students Have Diverse Abilities and Instructional Needs

Writing can be idiosyncratic, and this is reflected in how a student develops as a writer. At all grade levels, students show varying strengths and favor diverse forms (narrative, persuasive, expository, and so on), and often their writing gets worse before it improves. As Donald Murray, a Pulitzer Prize winner and professor emeritus of English at the University of New Hampshire, observes: "Most of us as writers have our strengths and our weaknesses. So do students. If you teach writing, you find people who are excellent spellers and understand the mechanics of grammar and don't say a thing. Others have voices. Some are very organized. Some are totally disorganized. I've taught first grade through graduate school. There's just an enormous range at every level."[4] For the teacher, the challenge is recognizing and then addressing the distinct instructional needs of diverse students.

Schools not only need to have students write more; they must also give students a rich and diverse array of writing experiences.

Students Must Master Diverse Writing Tasks to Develop Competence

A frequently stated goal of English language arts instruction is for the student to communicate competently and have the skills to participate in "varied literacy communities."[5] But what does competence in writing really mean? Across the grades, students write for varied purposes and audiences.

Educators may have distinct notions of competence in asking students to perform increasingly complex writing tasks. In early literacy, children's writing develops from drawing, talking, developmental spelling, and picture stories. In middle and high school, students may regularly be asked to write a summary, a lab report, a book review, or test essays of varying length and level of difficulty. In college, they are challenged with yet more complex and extended writing tasks for which they may not have been adequately prepared. To meet this challenge, schools not only need to have students write more; they must also give students a rich and diverse array of writing experiences.

Students Face Ongoing Challenges in Learning to Write

"Few people," wrote Mina Shaughnessy, "even among the most accomplished of writers, can comfortably say they have finished learning to write. . . . Writing is something writers are always learning to do." Working with so-called basic writers at the City College of New York, Shaughnessy was one of the first educators to draw attention to the logic of student writing errors and conflicting expectations about them in relation to mastering "school language." She observed that as student writers develop and are challenged with ever more difficult writing tasks, the number of mechanical errors and defects in their writing often increases. Spelling errors may give way to blunders in word choice, syntax, and rhetorical strategy. But errors of this kind can be misconstrued as regression rather than a sign of growth. Teachers, writes Mike Rose, should "analyze rather than simply criticize them. Error marks the place where education begins." Writing is never learned once and for all, and the effective writing teacher offers students the kind of response that supports their growth as writers.

Definitions of proficiency in writing vary widely from school to school and from teacher to teacher, with widest agreement at the lowest rung of the skills ladder, where correctness and basic readability are the concern, and the widest divergences at the upper rungs, where the stylistic preferences of teachers come into play. But even within the province of error, there are disagreements about the importance of different errors and about the number of errors an educated reader will tolerate without dismissing the writer as incompetent.

Mina Shaughnessy,
Errors and Expectations, p. 276

Teachers Need to Build
Common Expectations for Good Writing

If teachers within the same school have distinct or unexamined expectations for good writing, it can be confusing to students and a source of misunderstanding among faculty. Principals frequently cite teachers' varied assumptions about writing proficiency as a stumbling block for faculty in creating any schoolwide writing program. In the primary grades, where one teacher teaches all subjects, it may seem less of a hurdle, but the task of defining proficiency and making explicit expectations for good writing has to be addressed across all grade levels, content areas, and genres. As Crystal England, a former middle school principal, notes: "Only writing teachers are expected to teach writing across all subject areas. The science teachers may expect a well-researched, grammatically correct paper from new students, not realizing that for the six years before they got a particular child she never learned how to do that. So their whole perception of the child's writing and ability changes when they get those first works, and they blame the writing teachers, who, in turn, blame the earlier teachers. Every teacher who interacts with children has a responsibility for the student's development in writing as it applies to their subject area."[6]

We can no longer approach all writing with one set of criteria, assuming that one size fits all. It may be that, ultimately, we value some general qualities, such as "organization" or "quality of ideas." But we now know that the strategies that make good organization in a personal experience narrative may differ from the strategies that make a good report of information or a good persuasive letter. And we need to help students understand what those differences are, both by the way we teach and the way we evaluate their writing.

Charles Cooper and Lee Odell,
Evaluating Writing, p. xiii

Schools Need to Develop Fair and Authentic Writing Assessments

Student performance and growth in writing are difficult to measure not only because standards vary but also because a single-test assessment cannot show the range of a student's work or his or her development as a writer. Assessment of this kind may serve as a useful indicator of how well a school or district is doing with writing, but it is a limited instrument for diagnosing or evaluating a student's overall ability. Moreover, as recent studies[7] have shown, many state standards for writing are at variance with the rubrics or criteria used to assess it (see Chapter Five). As Grant Wiggins notes, "Many state writing assessments run the risk of undercutting good writing by scoring only for focus, organization, style, and mechanics without once asking judges to consider whether the writing is powerful, memorable, provocative, or moving (all impact-related criteria, and all at the heart of why people read what others write)."[8]

Educators Need Multiple Strategies for Teaching Writing

Because writing often involves complex thinking and problem solving, teachers need more than a set of fixed textbook procedures to teach it well and address the diverse needs of student writers. Historically, there has been tension between two distinct emphases in teaching composition: one that focuses on formal and external aspects of writing such as grammar, usage, sentence structure, and style; and another that focuses on meaning, ideas, expression, and writing processes. In most classrooms today, teachers draw from both approaches.[9]

Effective writing teachers address more than content only and more than just skills. In the classroom, the challenge comes in understanding *when* to focus on *which* aspect of writing. Although research-proven strategies for effective teaching exist (such as those described in Chapters Three and Four), they are most successfully applied by a teacher who can recognize and analyze a variety of student writing difficulties. Teaching writing well involves multiple teaching strategies that address both process *and* product, both form *and* content.[10]

> As school reform efforts are demonstrating, we must depend on reflective teachers as essential contributors to any national effort aimed at improving student achievement. Further, if schools are to become professional workplaces, writing will have to become integral to teachers' work and to their identities as professionals.
>
> Sarah W. Freedman, Linda Flower, Glynda Hull, and John R. Hayes, "Ten Years of Research: Achievements of the National Center for the Study of Writing and Literacy," p. 8

Schools Need to Offer Professional Development in Teaching Writing to All Faculty

First-hand experience with the practice of writing can help a teacher recognize the kinds of problems students have in improving their writing. According to Donald Graves, a writing researcher and professor of education at the University of New Hampshire, teachers still receive little instruction in teaching writing. Elementary school teacher training focuses on reading methods, and only a handful of states require a course in writing pedagogy for certification. Writing can support learning in all disciplines, including science and math, but relatively few high school instructors in those content areas have been exposed to research-proven, effective strategies for using it. In many schools, English teachers have the main responsibility for teaching writing. But districts and schools that have made writing an overarching curricular aim have done so by declaring it the job of all faculty and by providing ongoing professional development focused on writing. A key element in such systemic change is finding a core group of teachers who write and are enthusiastic about teaching it.

In many schools, English teachers have the main responsibility for teaching writing. But districts and schools that have made writing an overarching curricular aim have done so by declaring it the job of all faculty and by providing ongoing professional development focused on writing.

EVERYONE CAN LEARN TO WRITE

Improving writing requires a sustained schoolwide effort. On the one hand, it is hard to imagine an ability that is more desirable in academia and in the professional world than writing; on the other hand, many people believe writing is an elite talent, something only creative or literary people know how to do. This mystique goes against the success that many writing teachers have experienced with their students. A more hopeful credo is suggested in Peter Elbow's *Everyone Can Write:*

- It is possible for anyone to produce a lot of writing with pleasure and satisfaction and without too much struggle.

- It is possible for anyone to figure out what he or she really means and finally get it clear on paper.

- It is possible for anyone to write things that others will want to read.

- Teachers can empower students, help them to like to write, and be more forceful and articulate in using writing in their lives.[11]

Learning to Write

This chapter examines what research over the last three decades has learned about how writers compose and develop. Social and cognitive perspectives have transformed our understanding of the activity of writing and how it can be used in the classroom. Some of this research has focused on compositional processes and the practices of professional writers, and how these can be applied and developed in classrooms. Other research has focused on how literacy activities and communities outside the classroom influence children's learning in school. The chapter also explores the important link between reading and writing in early literacy development and what educators have learned about how young children use beginning, or so-called emergent, writing.

HOW WRITING WAS TAUGHT

Until the 1970s, most writing pedagogy emphasized learning and assessing a sequence of essential skills: forming letters, building vocabulary, identifying parts of speech, diagramming sentences, mastering grammar and punctuation, and following paragraph types and genres of writing according to prescribed conventions. This approach was largely product-centered and print-based; that is, it focused on the finished exemplar of student work with little or no attention to the purpose or process of producing it. The emphasis on correctness as "the most significant measure of accomplished prose" was rooted in a nineteenth-century model of language development[1] and a pedagogy of memorization and skill drills. It also assumed that reading should be taught before writing and that instruction in the latter should focus on extrinsic (linguistic and stylistic) conventions of writing and eradication of errors. Quantification and measurement of errors, as Rose notes, were central to the research methodology of the early twentieth century, but little attention was paid either to the social context of error or to "its significance in the growth of a writer."[2]

> *Emphasis on correctness was rooted in a nineteenth-century model of language development. Emphasis on mechanical errors overshadowed the deep rhetorical, social, and cognitive possibilities of writing for communication and critical thinking.*

Clearly, some skills emphasized in this approach embody knowledge that can help improve writing and understanding of language. But the scope of such writing instruction was limited. For one thing, it failed to distinguish between knowledge *about* language and experience with how language is used. Emphasis on mechanical errors overshadowed the deep rhetorical, social, and cognitive possibilities of writing for communication and critical thinking. This was a pedagogic view of writing not unlike the idea that a young person could learn to drive a car by memorizing state motoring laws and reading a repair manual. Undoubtedly, such texts might help a driver save on repairs, memorize rules of the road, and pass the written test, but that knowledge is no substitute for sitting behind the wheel and driving in a variety of conditions, preferably with an instructor in the passenger seat. Yet precisely this kind of thinking dominated the teaching of writing for much of the twentieth century. In a 1930 article for the *Eng-*

lish Journal, for example, Luella Cole Pressey proposed that "everything needed for about 90% of the writing students do . . . appears to involve only some 44 different rules of English composition." Her developmental scheme was mathematical: allocate the basics across grades two through twelve, so that "there is an average of 4.4 rules to be mastered per year."[3]

TEACHING WRITING AS PRODUCT

In many high school classrooms, variations on the product-centered approach to composition are still in use. Julie King, a middle school literacy consultant and teacher-coordinator with the Eastern Michigan Writing Project, describes how she was taught to write in high school:

> I can remember the class where we "learned to write." Each week we were given a five-hundred-word writing assignment. We wrote a variety of papers: narrative, descriptive, contrast-and-compare, and persuasive essays, to name a few. We would receive the assignment on Monday, with little discussion of what was expected. Sometimes we were given a few minutes to begin our papers, then we spent the rest of the week hearing about different types of sentences and paragraph unity. We never really applied those ideas to papers in class, but the teacher assumed we would use those skills correctly in our work. We did learn the "formula" for exposition: a three-part thesis with an introduction, three body paragraphs, and a conclusion. . . . The following Monday, she returned our papers with red marks and a grade on the last page. If we had over a certain number of red marks, we were required to recopy the incorrect sentences or misspelled words ten times.[4]

WRITING AS PROCESS

Researchers have long questioned the assumption that instruction in grammar, usage, and punctuation by itself will yield better writing. The issue was addressed in a groundbreaking 1985 National Institute of Education report, *Becoming a Nation of Readers:*

Instruction in grammar is often justified on the grounds that it improves students' writing. . . . However, it is a mistake to suppose that instruction in grammar transfers readily to the actual uses of language. This may be the explanation for the fact that experiments over the last fifty years have shown negligible improvements in the quality of student writing as a result of grammar instruction. Research suggests that the finer points of writing, such as punctuation and subject-verb agreement, may be learned best while students are engaged in extended writing that has the purpose of communicating a message to an audience. Notice that no communicative message is served when children are asked to identify on a worksheet the parts of speech or the proper use of *shall* and *will*.[5]

Decades of research[6] have shown that instructional strategies such as isolated skill drills fail to improve student writing. Beginning in the early 1970s, such researchers as Janet Emig and Donald Graves began looking into the question of how a writer actually worked at developing an individual piece of writing. Influenced by cognitive and sociocultural approaches to teaching and learning advanced by researchers such as Jean Piaget and Lev Vygotsky, they explored *processes* of composition—Emig by interviewing high school students and professional writers, and Graves by direct observation of young students writing.

Their work was driven by a need to understand the intellectual context of what it means to develop as a writer, what happens when people write, and how they learn to get better at it. The research identified phases and activities in the act of writing (planning, drafting, revision, editing). It also sought to understand where writing comes from: how a writer selects and limits a topic, and how writing moves from inchoate and vaguely defined thinking to more organized, coherent, and polished presentation of ideas and subject matter.

Subsequent research[7] found that writing could develop higher-order thinking skills: analyzing, synthesizing, evaluating, and interpreting. The very difficulty of writing is its virtue: it requires that students move beyond rote learning and simply reproducing information, facts, dates, and formulae. Students must also learn how to question their *own* assumptions and reflect critically on an alternative or an opposing viewpoint. From an instructional standpoint, argues George Hillocks, Jr., writing should be a form of inquiry. Compared with other pedagogic approaches, a writing curriculum that incorporates inquiry strategies (collecting and evaluating evidence, comparing and contrasting cases to infer similarities and differences, explaining how evidence supports or does not support a claim, creating a hypothetical example to clarify an idea, imagining a situation from a perspective other than one's own, and so on) has the most substantive and powerful impact on student performance.[8]

Inquiry-driven writing instruction has helped refocus attention on developing content in writing. Hillocks believes that composition teachers should help writers develop two kinds of procedural knowledge: inquiry strategies for developing the content of writing, and strategies for producing various kinds of written discourse.[9] These strategies are indispensable tools for critical literacy and the sort of academic discourse used in content areas. For example, a frequent complaint about student writing in secondary and postsecondary classes focuses on argument and the persuasive mode of writing. Common flaws are the use of a "chain of unsupported claims"; unclear support for an assertion; feelings masquerading as reason and evidence; and argument by assertion—that is, something is true because it's my opinion and I believe it strongly.

How can students be taught inquiry strategies that enable them to construct and sequence an authentic argument that engages them as thinkers and others as readers? Most students need models and some direct instruction to gain facility with this kind of writing. They also need the kind

> The writing process is anything a writer does from the time the idea came until the piece is completed or abandoned. There is no particular order. So it's not effective to teach writing process in a lock-step, rigid manner. What a good writing teacher does is help students see where writing comes from: in a chance remark or an article that really burns you up. I still hold by my original statement: if kids don't write more than three days a week, they're dead, and it's very hard to become a writer. If you provide frequent occasions for writing, then the students start to think about writing when they're not doing it. I call it a state of constant composition.
>
> Donald Graves,
> writing researcher and
> professor of education,
> University of New Hampshire

of scaffolding (an explicit framework or sequence of steps) in their assignments that gives them both an organizational scheme and guidelines for using inquiry strategies. Examples are described in an NAEP/ETS (Educational Testing Service) study of effective assignments (see Chapter Three). In his book *Engaging Ideas,* John C. Bean, director of Seattle University's writing program and an advocate of writing across the curriculum, suggests these ten strategies for teaching critical thinking and inquiry:

1. Think of tasks that would let students link concepts in your course to their personal experience or prior knowledge.

2. Ask students to teach difficult concepts in your course to a new learner.

3. Think of controversial theses in your field (for thesis-support assignments or believer-versus-doubter exercises).

4. Think of problems, puzzles, or questions you could ask students to address.

5. Give students raw data (such as lists, graphs, or tables) and ask them to write an argument or analysis based on the data.

6. Think of opening "frame" sentences for the start of a paragraph or short essay; students have to complete the paragraph by fleshing out the frame with generalizations and supporting detail.

7. Have students role-play unfamiliar points of view (imagine X from the perspective of Y) or what-if situations.

8. Select important articles in your field, and ask students to write summaries or abstracts of them.

9. Think of a controversy in your field, and ask students to write a dialogue between characters with different points of view.

10. Develop cases by writing scenarios that place students in realistic situations relevant to your discipline, where they must reach a decision to resolve a conflict.[10]

All of Bean's strategies can be presented in writing assignments adaptable to most grade levels and content areas. They can be used as the basis for in-class impromptu tasks, journals, letters, practice exams, multidraft formal assignments, small-group collaborative writing, or whole-class discussions.

The cognitive perspectives that have informed much educational research since the 1970s emphasized teaching students how to think and solve problems through logical reasoning and reflective critique in all subject areas. In writing, this perspective led to new models of how writers think when they compose. Most research today supports the view that writing is recursive,[11] that it does not proceed linearly but instead cycles and recycles through subprocesses that can be described this way:

1. Planning (generating ideas, setting goals, and organizing)

2. Translating (turning plans into written language)

3. Reviewing (evaluating and revising)[12]

Even for an experienced writer, the cycling occurs in no fixed order. Writers may create and change their goals as they move through these phases, depending on their topic, rhetorical purpose, and audience.

A mark of the writing process movement was that it grappled with the messiness of composing itself. Many writers don't know their subject well until they've written a draft; few professional writers start with a topic sentence or outline; and most struggle through multiple drafts and acts of editing and revision. As author Tracy Kidder has said, "I write because I don't know what I really think about anything until I get it down on paper."[13] Like him, many professional writers acknowledge that writing is never mastered once and for all; it is a lifelong, communicative mode of learning whose craft and processes must be adapted for distinct purposes and contexts. This notion of writing as inquiry, problem solving, and discovery has powerful implications for *all* learning: writing can deepen learn-

> Writing seems central to the shaping and directing of certain modes of cognition, is integrally involved in learning, is a means of defining the self and defining reality, is a means of representing and contextualizing information . . . and is an activity that develops over one's lifetime. . . . Writing is not just a skill with which one can present or analyze knowledge. It is essential to the very existence of certain kinds of knowledge.
>
> Mike Rose, quoted in Victor Villanueva, Jr. (ed.), *Cross-Talk in Composition Theory*, p. 533

A Glossary of Writing-as-Process Strategies

Audience Writers address real and imaginary audiences in their work. The audiences can include the writer himself or herself (as in a journal or diary), friends (letters, e-mails), a teacher, peers in school or the community, or a distant audience unknown to the writer. Students mature as writers by understanding how to write for different audiences, contexts, and purposes.

Writing processes Any of the activities or thinking strategies used to compose a piece of writing. These are sometimes described as cycles of planning (generating ideas, setting goals, and organizing), translating (putting a plan into writing) and reviewing (evaluating and revising); or they can be categorized as activities such as prewriting, drafting, revising, and editing.

Prewriting Any planning activity that helps the writer invent content and generate ideas, images, viewpoints, and so on, to be developed into a piece of writing. Methods include brainstorming, freewriting (see below), discussion, drawing, and role playing. Some writers follow up with organizational strategies such as grouping ideas and information into a web or cluster, or generating a preliminary outline. Correctness and mechanics are not the focus of a prewriting activity.

Freewriting Peter Elbow defines freewriting as private, nonstop writing—literally, putting words on paper continuously, without regard for the usual constraints of staying on topic or writing correctly. Such exploratory, unconstrained writing can help writers in moments when they feel stuck, blocked, or confused. Five or ten minutes of freewriting can help generate ideas, develop a free flow of thought, and energize writing. Many people practice it as a kind of warm-up exercise.

Drafting Here the writer begins to develop content through sustained production of connected prose. The number of drafts may depend on the type, length, and complexity of the writing task, but in an early draft mechanics and formal aspects of the writing are generally not emphasized. The goal is to begin to realize and shape the content of the piece in a form that allows the writer to explore and understand the territory of the subject. Writing may move from a "discovery draft" in rough form to a more focused presentation in which the material is shaped, organized, and structured in a final form for an authentic audience.

Revision In revising, a writer approaches a rough draft with an editorial eye, identifying and deleting extraneous subject matter, focusing the material, determining what needs to be amplified and what needs to be cut. Revising involves structural changes to a text, or macro editing—refining content and creating structure by organizing ideas and themes into sequenced, coherent paragraphs. Writers need to learn revision strategies, and teachers can help by modeling the process, showing drafts of their own or someone else's writing and demonstrating how revision can transform and clarify a piece of writing. Students then learn that writing is a continual process of revising or re-seeing their work.

Editing In *Teaching with Writing* (p. 75), Toby Fulwiler defines editing as "the process which makes sure that you say exactly what you mean to say in the most appropriate language possible." For some teachers and writers, editing is synonymous with revision. For others, it is micro editing—that is, line edits and proofreading at the level of the sentence or phrase or word, focusing on mechanics, spelling, punctuation, and other conventions. Editing prepares a piece of writing for its final or published form.

Peer response A classroom technique designed to help the student develop editing skills and a sense of authentic audience. The teacher first models a process of supportive critique that sets the tone for positive and useful comments. Students then read and review one another's work in pairs or groups, soliciting critical feedback as they present their writing to peers. The student learns to serve as a critical friend and audience for another's work, offering suggestions for revision. Reading aloud also helps student writers develop an ear for wordiness, awkward construction, and omissions. (For a classroom example, see the Sherry Swain classroom vignette later in this chapter.)

Inquiry strategies As defined by George Hillocks, Jr., in *The Testing Trap,* inquiry strategies include comparing and contrasting cases to develop inferences about similarity and difference, explaining how evidence supports or does not support a claim, collecting and evaluating evidence, imagining a situation from a perspective other than one's own, and so on. These thinking strategies are the same ones the writer needs to produce content. They can be practiced in discussion and developed in writing.

Sentence combining An instructional technique designed to help students improve syntactic fluency and vary or expand their repertoire of sentence patterns. In its simplest form, students take two or more short sentences and combine them into one longer, complex, or compound sentence. In more developed forms, the student might create a more complex pattern, such as parallelism, through imitation of a model.

Writing portfolio A collection of student works in a folder or binder that allows a student to reflect on his or her growth as a writer and allows a teacher to assess progress. It may include multiple drafts of a piece, a student's self-selected best work, or a collection that shows a range of written work in several genres. Extended portfolios frequently include a self-reflection piece by the student surveying personal progress and future goals as a writer. In some states (Kentucky, for example), writing is assessed through portfolios (see Chapter Five).

Writing across the curriculum Using writing in many content areas introduces students to the conventions and literacies of various discourse communities, including rules of evidence, terminology, and writing forms. Advocates of writing across the curriculum believe that writing can be a tool for learning in all disciplines. Some, like Bean (whose strategies have already been presented in this chapter), view writing as both "a process of doing critical thinking and a product communicating the results of critical thinking" (*Engaging Ideas,* p. 3). Writing can thus develop habits of inquiry, exploration, and interpretation applicable to all disciplines.

ing not just in a literature class but also in mathematics, science, history, and the arts.

Research into writing processes remains enormously influential to the teacher's practice. Students in a good writing teacher's classroom—whether in kindergarten or in college—engage in inquiry, drafting, revising, and editing. As important as this research is to the writing teacher, it could not answer some fundamental questions facing schools in the 1980s. The increasing diversity of school-age children (especially but not exclusively in urban centers) raised new questions about culture and schooling. Shirley Brice Heath's *Ways with Words*[14] showed how the written and oral language habits of African American and low-income families often did not mesh well with the literacy requirements of the school. The absence of success for these children did not stem from any lack of cognitive ability but from misperceptions between home and school cultures. Heath's study and others initiated what John Trimbur called "the social turn" in writing instruction.

> Teachers can have students write to discover, create and explore their thinking, dig up prior knowledge, to cultivate intellectual independence, to conjecture about possibilities, to struggle with difficult concepts, and to engage the imagination as an ally in learning.
>
> Tom Romano, *Clearing the Way: Working with Teenage Writers*, p. 34

Much of the sociocultural research from this era focused on conflict and continuity between home and school literacy. Many of these findings were surprising. Denny Taylor and Catherine Dorsey-Gaines found that the home literacy practices of an urban African American family were rich and varied, including a great deal of both reading and writing. Their children's difficulties in school were often due to factors such as housing and poverty or inadequate school programs.[15]

This research was important because it brought new respect to students' language, even if that language differed, in some cases, from the language of school. It was an important reminder that language use isn't solely a thinking activity, but also a social and cultural act. Literacy, as James Paul Gee argues, involves more than simply learning to read and write. Student writing develops within a context of discourse—that is, a system of values, beliefs, norms, and behaviors that is inherently social. Student writing and reading makes up part of their "identity kit," composed of ways of "saying-writing-valuing-believing" that is evident not only in the language of school children but in the language practices that mark the identities of doctors, educators, steelworkers, and mechanics.

The emphasis on culture and identity has helped educators more effectively and sensitively teach children who are also English language learners. ELL studies from the last decade observe that learning a new language, in addition to being a grammatical task, also asks the student to take on a new identity. Writing instruction succeeds when the new identity of the student does not oppose home culture. Freeman and Freeman sum up the lesson from this research: "Effective school programs take into account factors from both the school and the societal contexts in planning curriculum for language minority students."[16]

The ability to consider factors from both "the school and the societal contexts" is perhaps the main lesson of the "social turn." Writing research has shown us that learning to write involves not only learning the processes of inquiry, drafting, revising, and editing, but also a web of relationships between a child and her peers, home life and the wider culture, or a child's culture and that of the school. This research suggests that the best writing teaching simultaneously supports the child's home identity while promoting success in school.

> We must think of literacy (or literacies) as particular ways of using language for a variety of purposes, as a sociocultural practice with intellectual significance.
>
> Luis Moll, "Literacy Research in Community and Classrooms," p. 237

HOW (AND WHEN) CHILDREN LEARN TO WRITE

Historically, early literacy development in schools was premised on the idea that reading should be taught before writing, a view that persisted well into the 1960s. The educator, says P. David Pearson, an early-reading specialist and dean of the Graduate School of Education at the University of California, Berkeley, assumed that "presenting young children with two tasks would be too much." But writing, Pearson argues, can play a central role in early reading development. His views are supported by the National Research Council's report *Preventing Reading Difficulties in Young Children*.[17] What Pearson calls the "synergistic relationship" between learning to read and learning to write makes it crucial to teach writing from kindergarten on (see the commentary by Pearson later in this chapter). Other reasons for teaching it in the early grades are suggested from observation of how young children use their beginning writing. Anne Haas Dyson's studies of early literacy development[18] have shown how children use "print to represent their ideas and to interact with other people"[19] when they scribble; draw and label pictures; and create, act out, or retell stories. Children can express ideas in writing even "before they have mastered all the mechanics of standard orthography, sentence and paragraph structure. Educators and researchers working from this view also explain that writing instruction begins in pre-school and includes generating content for purposes of discovery, self expression, and communication."[20]

Very young children draw and talk to explore and develop their use of print. As Dyson and Freedman observe, "They understand that writing, like drawing, is a way of representing experiences. Children may, in fact, view writing as similar to drawing in the way that meaning is encoded in both. That is, they may view writing as direct symbolism: children may not form letters to represent speech, but to represent known people, objects, or the names of those figures directly."[21]

Children's writing development is linked as well to social practices around them and their discovery that language has social and practical purposes. For example, "as elementary school teachers follow the suggestions of . . . recent writing research, they begin to direct children to write to real audiences,

---

Although we have a sense of what "effective" and "ineffective" classrooms are like [from Donald Graves's *Writing: Teachers and Children at Work* and *Balance the Basics: Let Them Write*], with a population as diverse as our own we need to understand the social and cognitive dimensions of classroom activities and how children with different literacy backgrounds and understandings react to these activities. Only then will we understand the features we can manipulate as we work to create more comfortable and effective classrooms for all our students.

Sarah W. Freedman, Anne Haas Dyson, Linda Flower, and Wallace Chafe, "Research in Writing," p. 4

From the standpoint of the child, the great waste in school comes from his inability to utilize the experiences he gets outside of the school in any complete and free way within the school itself; while, on the other hand, he is unable to apply in daily life what he is learning in school.

John Dewey, quoted in Glynda Hull and Katherine Schultz, *School's Out!,* p. 3

with a genuine reason to share ideas, and to rely on audiences, such as classmates and teachers, for feedback and evaluation regarding successive drafts."[22] Writing then becomes a springboard for children to communicating and developing their ideas and to accepting different points of view.

These perspectives on early literacy reflect a new understanding of how reading and writing are "intertwined and inseparable language tools" throughout a student's learning.[23] One review of fifty years of correlational and experimental studies investigating reading and writing relationships concluded that

- Better writers tend to be better readers (of their own writing as well as of other reading material).

- Better writers tend to read more than poorer writers.

- Better readers tend to produce more syntactically mature writing than poorer readers.[24]

Children appear to move across various forms of writing even up to grade 1, using scribble, nonphonetic letter strings, and drawing as forms of writing from which they subsequently read. They plan their compositions to various degrees and respond to adults who ask them what they plan to write. They tend to hold to a plan and then read back consistent with that plan at this age, even though the writing cannot be read by another conventionally. As children become more proficient writers, they often go through a period or periods of insisting on "writing it the right way," asking for conventional spellings.

National Research Council, *Preventing Reading Difficulties in Young Children*, pp. 69–70

THE READING-WRITING CONNECTION

How does writing support reading development? In *Literacy for the Twenty-First Century: A Balanced Approach,* Gail E. Tompkins, professor of literacy and early education and director of the San Joaquin Valley Writing Project at California State University, Fresno, argues that writing helps children's reading development in three ways:

1. *Readers and writers use the same intellectual strategies.* These include organizing, monitoring, questioning, and revising meaning. Children grow in their ability to use these strategies through both reading and writing activity. The biggest difference between good and poor readers and good and poor writers is their strategy use, not their skill use.

Reading development does not take place in isolation; instead, a child develops simultaneously as reader, listener, speaker, and writer. The research has led many educators to agree that integrating reading and writing has multiple benefits for development of literacy.

2. *The reading and writing processes are similar.* The first step in both processes, for example, involves activating prior knowledge and setting a purpose. Because the two processes are so similar, the student learns literacy concepts and procedures through both reading and writing.

3. *Children use many of the same skills in both reading and writing.* Phonics is a good example of this transfer. Children use phonics skills to decode words in becoming fluent readers, and they also use phonics knowledge to "sound out" the spelling of words and apply spelling rules.[25]

Numerous studies and assessments, including the NAEP 1998 Reading Report Card, have shown that reading development does not take place in isolation; instead, a child develops simultaneously as reader, listener, speaker, and writer. The research has led many educators to agree that integrating reading and writing has multiple benefits for development of literacy.[26]

P. DAVID PEARSON

The Synergies of Writing and Reading in Young Children

As dean of the Graduate School of Education at the University of California, Berkeley, P. David Pearson is widely recognized for his research in reading and literacy evaluation. He has also served as co-director of two nationally prominent literacy research institutes: the Center for the Study of Reading at the University of Illinois and Michigan State University's Center for the Improvement of Early Reading Achievement. Interviewed for this publication, Pearson describes some synergies of reading and writing and the implications for developing literacy in classrooms.

Writing has a central role in early reading development. Increasingly, we see the synergistic relationship between learning to write and learning to read. At the most rudimentary level, when kids are encouraged to write, even at a very early age, prekindergarten and kindergarten, and they're encouraged to spell words as they sound them, two things happen. The first is that they develop phonemic awareness in precisely the way that the advocates of direct phonemic instruction intend for it to be learned and tested. But with writing, they do it, I would argue, in a much more incidental, less laborious, and more natural way. And it's acquired in the service of some other functional task—namely, trying to communicate something with someone.

A second synergy is that there's actually some payoff in terms of the letter-sound knowledge—the kind you use to sound out words while reading, even though we all know that when you're writing and trying to spell things the way they sound you're not going from the letter to sound, you're going from the sound to letter. But there's enough of an overlap between these two correspondences that transfer occurs. Phonics is so much more transparent in spelling than it is in reading that I think it's easier for kids to deal with.

Less obvious are the more structural and conceptual kinds of symmetry. For example, when you engage kids in writing stories there's a natural hookup to those they have been reading. This may be an instance where the writing helps kids. Because it's surely the case that kids use the stories they read as models for their writing. But it also works back the other way—from writing to reading. Because the minute the student now uses a story frame that he or she gathers from the stories that have been read with someone, the student can now use that structural idea in writing in a more vivid way. The minute the student uses some sort of story frame in her writing, it becomes a potential object for deliberate examination. Writing makes things concrete and puts it out there for inspection in a way that reading doesn't. And when a student has to deal with "once upon a time" and "they lived happily ever after" in writing, it hits her in the face more than in reading. And that helps the next time she encounters one of the frames in reading.

Another way to look at this is that when you're writing, it slows things down so you can examine the language. We've discovered this in some of our work with ESL learners. Written language makes language available for examination in a way that oral language doesn't. If I want to examine carefully the way language is used, then having it available in print makes it easier. And when I write, that examination is made even more concrete than when I read.

The strategies that are part of learning to write, such as peer editing and author's chair, also help kids with reading. When I do a peer editing, I'm asking questions like, "OK, what was it you really wanted to say?" and "How well did you say it?" and "How could I help you say it better?" And these are exactly the kind of questions we are trying to promote in critical reading: getting to the author, trying to understand the author's intentions and motives. Why in heaven's name would someone say this? And why would they say it in the way they did? So for me when you engage kids in this kind of peer editing, you're engaging in the first steps of critical reading. That's another one of those important synergies that isn't often talked about.

Another obvious synergy is that the texts that we write in a classroom are potentially texts for you and me and our peers to read to one another. That's a wonderful kind of expectation to promote in classrooms: what we write is written to be read. They're not written to satisfy my assignments as a teacher. It implies that the criterion of authenticity is going to be important inside classrooms. And by authenticity I mean purpose—that it's written to be read by a real person other than a teacher.

So these are synergies that link learning to read and learning to write: the first at a letter-sound level, the second at a structural level, and the third one less structural and more about the pragmatics of language intention and purpose and the relation to an audience. If I were asked to offer advice on building a reading-and-language arts program for grade one or even kindergarten, I would have writing time every day. It might be ten or fifteen minutes to start with. Students would be composing texts: some on their own, some with buddies, and some with a group. I would use a combination of individual texts, small-group texts, and the more conventional language experience stories—all those to me should be part of a reading-writing program.

CLASSROOM VIGNETTE
The Reading-Writing Connection in Mississippi

Sherry Swain, director of the Mississippi Writing/Thinking Institute at Mississippi State University, describes how she combines reading, writing, and talking about literature in her first-grade classroom.

After my first graders write about their reading in their journals, they read what they've written out loud, three times. As they do that, I observe and make notes. And as they read aloud, they catch words that they have left out, and I see them begin to erase and make changes. So there's a little bit of self-revision, plus preparing to read aloud to an audience, and some editing. Then we go into a circle, and the children read what they had written to the group. When the kids share this reading, there are conversations about the book being funny or how it reminds them of another book or a personal experience. In the process, children have begun to learn different ways of responding to reading.

One is the critical response—when we talk about how a book has a lot of rhyme in it. Another is the personal connection, the connection to other literature, or "what I learned from this book." A teacher can make a list from the kids' conversations of the ways people respond to literature. And then a teacher can ask, "Is there anybody who's never written a summary?" Or "Anyone who's never written about the author's style?" A teacher can begin to push the kids to try out new types of response, so they're not always saying, "This is my book. I like my book." That's what I call a reading-writing connection.

INTEGRATING CONTENT, PROCESS, AND SKILLS

Enthusiasm for writing-as-process strategies led some to embrace the approach as a panacea for what *Newsweek* in 1975 called America's "writing crisis."[27] But today, even proponents of writing-as-process (such as Donald Graves) acknowledge that their research prompted educators to fashion rigidly sequenced writing process curricula: a day of freewriting, another class on drafting, followed by a workshop on editing, and so on, followed by a final draft. But there is no *one* writing process, Graves argues. Writers need to discover what works best for them in a variety of writing tasks. A second misapplication of the writing-as-process approach was that "the basics"—the mechanics and finer points of writing—did not matter; students could learn them on their own. In his book *The English Teacher's Companion*, Jim Burke, a high school English teacher in

Burlingame, California, and founder of CATEnet (an electronic round-table designed to promote discussion among English teachers around the country), describes the problem:

> States throughout the country are drafting legislation for curriculum standards and frameworks that calls for renewed emphasis on the teaching of grammar (or what is sometimes called "conventions"). This demand stems from a frustration in the workplace and [in] college writing programs with students' lack of grammatical correctness, a problem that some believe derives from those teachers who say "grammar doesn't matter" when kids are writing, a remark we should never make. What we can tell our students, however, is that at the preliminary stage of their writing they need to concentrate on developing their ideas, and that we can look at their grammar and conventions later, when they revise and edit. Even this is not enough, however; if students aren't regularly held accountable for their correctness, it just won't seem important to them. Imagine a math class where it "doesn't matter if you get it right. . . . " The argument has always been that knowing grammar does not improve your writing and thus its study serves no purpose. If, however, students learn elements of grammar in the context of expanding their options as writers, it has its place. It also has a place in the curriculum as a tool for thinking about relationships, patterns, and logic.[28]

From another perspective, Lisa Delpit has questioned superficial application of both the process and the product approaches—particularly with reference to the instructional needs of minority students. Delpit has focused on the phenomenon of "underteaching": the practice of "teaching down" to minority children on the part of educators who do not want to strain what they see as these students' low ability. Underteaching, writes Delpit, can result from *either* a skills-based or a process approach to writing. On the one hand, she argues, focusing on decontextualized and isolated skills can be boring and meaningless for low-scoring students, especially when they are pummeled with drill-based instruction that offers them no chance "to use their minds and interpret texts."[29] On the other hand, when process-oriented instruction focuses on "finding a voice" or endless drafts to the exclusion of producing a final product, minority students may never learn the basics of standard English—the gatekeeper and language of power all students need to master. Agreeing that writing instruction should focus on authentic writing tasks—that is, writing with purpose and for a real audience—Delpit criticizes those who view direct instruction of basic skills as "repressive" or who believe that teaching standard English devalues the home languages of linguistically diverse students:

> Skills are a necessary but insufficient aspect of black and minority students' education. Students need technical skills to open doors, but they need to be able to think critically and creatively in meaningful and potentially liberating work inside those doors. Let there be no doubt: a "skilled" minority person who is not also capable of critical analysis becomes the trainable, low-level functionary of the dominant society, simply the grease that keeps the institutions which orchestrate his or her oppression running smoothly. On the other hand, a critical thinker who lacks the "skills" demanded by employers and institutions of higher learning can aspire to financial and social status only within the disenfranchised underworld. Yes, if minority students are to effect change which will allow them to truly progress, we must insist on "skills" within the context of critical and creative thinking.[30]

The question of direct or explicit instruction carries over to learning more complex literacy tasks, whether they involve mastering the conventions of academic discourse or understanding Shakespearean prosody. Delpit and others have stressed the importance of building on the literacy skills and expertise that minority students bring to the classroom. Such an approach emphasizes these teaching principles:

• The culture and literacy of the students are seen as a springboard to wider knowledge.

- A student's dialect or home language is respected and used as a tool for teaching conventions and forms of standard English.
- Basic skills and mechanics are integrated with the study of writing and literature.

Delpit describes how one Native Alaskan teacher, Martha Demientieff, dealt with her Athabaskan students' difficulty with "book language" by exploring differences between it and their own language:

> The students discuss how book language always uses more words, but how in Heritage language, brevity is always best. Students then work in pairs, groups, or individually to write papers in an academic way, discussing with Martha and with each other whether they believe they have said enough to "sound like a book." Next they take those papers and try to reduce the meaning to a few sentences. Finally, students further reduce the message to a "saying" brief enough to go on the front of a T-shirt, and the sayings are put on little paper T-shirts that the students cut out and hang throughout the room. Sometimes the students reduce other authors' wordy texts to their essential meanings as well. Thus, through winding back and forth through orality and literacy, the students begin to understand the stylistic differences between their own language and standard text.[31]

THE CHANGING LANDSCAPE OF WRITING INSTRUCTION

In the 1980s, when Arthur Applebee conducted studies of the status of writing in American schools,[32] he found that in general students "wrote infrequently within a narrow range of genres for limited purposes." Most of it involved "writing without composing: fill in the blank and completion exercises, direct translation, or other seat work in which the text was instructed by the teacher or textbook, and the student supplied missing information that was, typically, judged as right or wrong."[33] Compared with the penmanship exercises of the nineteenth century, some might call this progress, but such instruction still reflects a low level of expectation of writing and does not prepare students for complex writing and thinking tasks. Some improvement, however, is suggested by evidence from more recent national assessments of writing by NAEP: "By 1998, 57 percent or more of the teachers also were reporting that writing process instruction and integrated reading and writing were central to their teaching, and another 51 percent reported similar emphasis on grammar and skill-based instruction. Rather than treating writing process approaches and skill-based instruction as in opposition to one another, all but a handful of teachers reported some emphasis on both."[34]

An example of a middle school teacher who successfully combines both approaches is Gail Slatko, whose classrooms were featured in a set of research reports and case studies for CELA, the National Research Center on English Learning and Achievement.[35]

CLASSROOM VIGNETTE
A Classroom That Beat the Odds

Gail Slatko teaches in Florida's Ruben Dario Middle School, whose student population is 83 percent Hispanic, 12 percent African American, and 4 percent white. "Although only 14 percent are officially designated as LEP [limited English proficiency] most Ruben Dario students do not speak English as their first language."[36] This high-performing school, "located in a high-crime area," successfully serves some of the poorest students in the state. "Ruben Dario students . . . score well above the state standard on the mandated Florida Writes! Exam."[37]

Slatko combines various activities to help her students become better readers, writers, and editors. For example, she often teaches vocabulary skills within the context of literature and writing, but she also asks students to complete practice workbook exercises designed to increase their vocabulary. They create a "living dictionary" by collecting new words as they come across them in books, magazines, and newspapers. To give practice with analogies,

Because Writing Matters

Slatko goes beyond merely providing examples; she requires that students discuss their response and explain the rationale for their answer. Later, students design a vocabulary mobile, which she displays in the classroom. She uses the same approach when she targets literary concepts, conventions, and language. Students integrate literary and vocabulary learning when they create children's books, incorporating vocabulary, alliteration, and storytelling through words and pictures. During one recent school year, five books were entered in the county fair competition, and one of them was awarded first prize. Slatko's lessons are a model for her students to use in their own reading and writing as well as when they are editing and responding to writing.[38]

Using multiple lesson types, Slatko teaches by mixing process and product approaches. Her practice uses these teaching strategies:

- *Students learn skills and mechanics within the context of literature and writing.* She combines targeted skills instruction (workbook exercises) with integrated activities (living dictionary).

- *Students develop peer editing skills on the basis of teacher modeling.* She offers "overt, targeted instruction and review as models for peer and self-evaluation."[39]

- *Students write for a real audience.* Student work is discussed among peers and then published and disseminated in a real-world context.

Tailored to the needs of her particular group of students, Slatko's integration of process and product approaches is a model and a success story, one with many variations in classrooms where students are effectively learning to write. The next chapter explores other effective practices and the power of writing when used in content-rich subject areas—what is sometimes called "writing to learn."

Writing to Learn

This chapter examines what recognized national assessments have revealed about strategies that help students improve their writing. What does research identify as the most promising teaching strategies and practices? It also presents a case study showing how writing supports or advances learning in diverse subject areas. The assessment findings suggest a pair of larger, more complex questions: Can these same writing strategies be transferred to subject areas such as math and science, where content is king? Why does learning to write also mean writing to learn? The chapter concludes by exploring the importance of incorporating critical thinking and inquiry in the teaching of writing.

NATIONAL WRITING ASSESSMENTS

Part of what we know about what helps students learn to write comes from published analyses of writing assessments. The most recent and widely cited study of writing achievement levels of American students is the 1998 National Assessment of Educational Progress (NAEP) report card on writing, published by the U.S. Department of Education.[1] The NAEP report linked student performance in grades four, eight, and twelve to various home and school practices. Among the practices cited by students who outperformed their peers or who received higher average scores were the following:

- *Planning.* "Those students [at grades 8 and 12] who were asked to plan their writing at least once a week or once or twice a month outperformed their peers who were never or hardly ever asked to do so."
- *Multiple Drafts.* "While there were no relationships with student scores at grade 4, students at grades 8 and 12 who reported being asked to write more than one draft . . . had higher average scores than their peers who were not asked to do so."

The NAEP report also suggests that two teacher practices support higher scores in writing:

- *Teacher-Student Discussion.* "A positive relationship was evident between teachers talking with students about what students were writing and students' writing scores. This was more evident at grades 8 and 12 than at grade 4; at grades 8 and 12, students whose teachers always spoke with them about their writing outperformed their peers whose teachers sometimes spoke with them about their writing."
- *Portfolios.* "There was a positive relationship at all three grades between student writing scores and students saving or having their work saved in folders or portfolios."

Other NAEP assessments have underscored the interrelationship of writing and reading comprehension and the importance of increased frequency and length of writing assignments in classrooms. They suggest the value for writing across the curriculum as well.

The NAEP report also suggests that two teacher practices support higher scores in writing: (1) teacher-student discussion and (2) portfolios. Other NAEP assessments have underscored the interrelationship of writing and reading comprehension and the importance of increased frequency and length of writing assignments.

Writing Long Answers to Questions

Students in the NAEP 1998 reading assessment were asked how frequently in school they wrote long answers in response to test questions or reading assignments. The following figure shows the frequency with which students wrote long answers and the corresponding average score. Students who reported engaging in this activity weekly or monthly had higher average scores than students who reported doing so only once or twice a year or less.

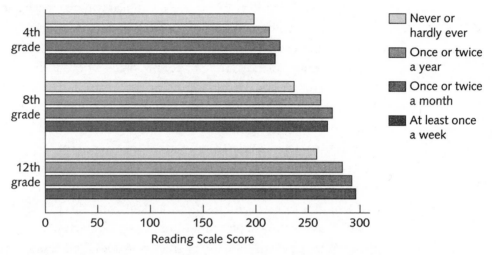

Reading Scale Score

Legend:
- Never or hardly ever
- Once or twice a year
- Once or twice a month
- At least once a week

Reading Scores, by Frequency of Writing Long Answers to Questions That Involved Reading, 1998

Source: S. White, *The NAEP 1998 Reading Report Card: National and State Highlights.* (NCES 1999-479). Washington, D.C.: National Center for Education Statistics, U.S. Department of Education, 1999.

NAEP's 1998 findings also confirmed earlier assessments of the role of writing-as-process strategies. Using data from its 1992 writing assessment, another NAEP report[2] found that "teaching the cluster of writing techniques known collectively as 'writing process' is associated with higher average writing proficiency among students. Students whose teachers always had them do such activities, especially in combination, had the highest average writing scores. Students who did certain pre-writing activities on the actual NAEP test also had higher average proficiency scores than other students."

The same NAEP report defined *process-oriented instruction* as one that approached writing as "problem-solving," offering students a broad range of strategies such as prewriting, defining the audience, and "planning the writing, as well as drafting and revising." It quoted a much-cited research review by George Hillocks showing that "weaker writers spend little time planning, while skilled writers do more planning and reviewing. More skilled writers, furthermore, pay more attention to content and organization, while weaker writers are more preoccupied with the mechanics of writing, especially spelling. Good writers are found to use a longer pre-writing period than average writers."[3]

Thus, writing practices are an important predictor of student performance.

The NAEP findings reflect a growing consensus in the field about what the student can do as a writer and what the teacher can do in the classroom to support improved writing and learning. However, despite broad infusion of process strategies in classrooms across the nation, concern remains as to the quality of their implementation and why they seem to work better with some students and in some classrooms than with others.[4] Although the NAEP findings are a useful resource in identifying effective teaching strategies such as portfolios, planning, and revision of writing, their actual application in the classroom varies greatly, as does their impact at different grade levels.

Two subsequent studies provide growing evidence for what the teacher can do in the classroom to support high-quality writing. They give precise description and analysis of specific, successful classroom strategies. One, prepared for NAEP by the Educational Testing Service and the National Writing Project, focused on key features of effective writing assignments.[5] A second, conducted by the Academy for Educational Development, studied practices of NWP teachers in a group of third- and fourth-grade classrooms in five states.[6]

A STUDY OF EFFECTIVE WRITING ASSIGNMENTS

For teachers, an important aspect of curriculum that can influence student performance is the quality of writing assignments. The ETS/NAEP study analyzed writing assignments from thirty-five fourth-grade and twenty-six eighth-grade classrooms selected from a 1998 NAEP writing study. These assignments all had produced strong writing (on the basis of performance in the NAEP assessment) from at least two-thirds of the students. The analysis combined reviews of student writing with teacher interviews and student description of the assignments. The study found that effective writing assignments encourage student engagement with writing processes in ways that go beyond formulaic use of prewriting, drafting, and revision. They do so by their use and balance of four key elements:

Content and Scope

An effective assignment does more than ask students to write about what they have read or experienced. It engages students in a series of cognitive processes, such as reflection, analysis, and synthesis, so that they are required to transform the information from the reading material or other sources in order to complete the writing assignment.

> *An effective writing assignment does more than ask students to write about what they have read or experienced. It engages students in a series of cognitive processes, such as reflection, analysis, and synthesis, so that they are required to transform the information from the reading material in order to complete the writing assignment.*

A successful assignment might ask students to read a story and compare the motivation of two characters. Students would then have to select information from the story and apply it by analyzing motives. By contrast, an assignment that asks students to read a story and describe only one of the characters invites a weaker response: the student need only locate the information and restate it.

Organization and Development

An effective assignment gives students a framework for developing ideas and organizational guidelines that help them analyze and synthesize the information with which they are working.

Two common deficiencies of writing assignments are weak guidelines for structuring ideas and lack of appropriate scaffolding. For example, a typical fourth-grade assignment—"Describe your bedroom; use specific details"—provides no guidelines for the student to work with. The ETS/NAEP study's research team suggested how such an assignment might be strengthened: "Describe your bedroom for a classmate who hasn't seen it. Your description should include enough detail so that when a classmate reads it, s/he will be able to tell what you like, what your interests are, and what's important to you. In fact, from reading the description, classmates should be able to identify you as the resident of that room. Descriptions will be posted for your classmates to read."

Audience and Communication

An effective assignment goes beyond the use of a "pretend" audience and offers the student a genuine opportunity to communicate to a real audience. For example, an assignment asking students to explain a process is a staple of many writing classes. A typical eighth-grade assignment asks students to write to the teacher explaining how to open a school locker. But the student knows that the teacher already knows how to do it. A more effective approach might ask students to identify an area of expertise (tying a fishing fly or collecting baseball cards) not shared by the reader and then explain something to that audience on the basis of the writer's unique experience, knowledge, and perspective.

Engagement and Choice

An effective assignment avoids the pitfalls of offering the student too much choice or none at all. Restricting the range of decisions that the student is asked to make is a way for her to increase engagement in the assignment.

An effective fourth-grade assignment that invites such engagement and choice while connecting all four of these features asks the student to "interview an older person at home and write the results of the interview in paragraphs. Include the facts about the person's childhood, young adulthood, and mature adulthood. Include a description of what a typical day would be for this person at each of three stages of life and how the interviewee had fun."

A STUDY OF NWP CLASSROOM PRACTICES

A 2002 report to the National Writing Project by the Academy for Educational Development (AED) studied thirty-five third- and fourth-grade classrooms of writing project teachers in five states (Mississippi, Oklahoma, Pennsylvania, Kentucky, and California). This three-year study was designed to collect data on how student writing is developed, what conditions support achievement in writing, and student outcomes in those classrooms.

Time Spent on Writing Activities

NWP teachers spend far more time on writing instruction than most fourth-grade teachers across the country. Eighty-three percent of NWP classroom teachers in the AED study spent more than ninety minutes per week on writing activities, compared with just 31 percent of fourth-grade teachers nationally.

Breadth of Writing Activities

There was an enormous range and diversity of writing in NWP classrooms. Of forty-five assignments analyzed in the first year of the AED study, eighteen involved expository tasks, ten were personal or family narratives, eight were creative writing, five were poetry assignments, and four included persuasive writing.

Writing Strategies

For students in NWP classrooms, writing is an ongoing, daily practice. Most assignments used these writing process strategies: pair or group work (87 percent), peer editing (69 percent), completing multiple drafts (84 percent), and conferencing with students (78 percent).

The participating institutions included urban, rural, and suburban public schools. In three-fourths of the schools studied, more than half the students were eligible for free or reduced-price lunches, and data were collected from a total of 763 students. The AED report included findings about NWP teachers' strategies and classrooms (see box on p. 49).

I use writing throughout the day—it is part of almost everything. The children write to explain and write to integrate what they've learned in different areas. . . . When I plan what I do [in any subject], I always plan a writing component.

A fourth-grade NWP teacher in the AED study

Much of the AED report focused on "authentic intellectual work," defined as original application of knowledge and skills rather than routine use of facts and procedures[7] and the emphasis teachers place on such work in their assignments. Research shows that teachers who give students assignments requiring authentic intellectual work see greater gains on standardized tests.[8] Such work resembles the kind of problem solving that adults face in their everyday lives and helps prepare the student to be a critical, analytical thinker. In assignments, it means asking the student to construct knowledge through analysis, synthesis, and interpretation.

Among examples of authentic intellectual work in NWP classrooms, the AED study cited two descriptions of fourth-grade writing assignments. The first asked students to demonstrate an understanding of concepts ("story line and character development"). In the second assignment, students completed a "changes of state" expository essay in science, and the sample student response demonstrated what the AED study termed "substantial construction of knowledge" as the student analyzed, synthesized, or interpreted content.[9] Here is how the teachers described their assignments:

CLASSROOM VIGNETTES
NWP Fourth-Grade Writing Assignments

Assignment 1: We were working on the story *Charlotte's Web*. I asked my students to put themselves in the author's shoes and attempt to produce a new final chapter with a clear story line and substantial detail to support characters, setting, problem, and conclusion. I asked them to use dialogue and quotation marks.

Assignment 2: Our class studied changes of state for two months. Five months later, I gave the class this question for review: a student had three cups of water. She poured one cup into a shallow pie plate. She left one cup of water in the cup. She poured a third cup of water into a tall graduated cylinder. She left these containers on a shelf and counted the days before each container was empty. Here are the results:

• Water in the pie plate was gone in 4 days.
• Water in the glass was gone in 14 days.
• Water in the graduated cylinder was gone in 160 days.

Discuss what was done. What was the student trying to learn about? What were the reasons for the results?

As these examples show, writing can be used for a high level of learning in a variety of content areas.

WRITING TO LEARN ACROSS THE CURRICULUM

As instructional leaders, school administrators can play a vital role in ensuring that writing is used to achieve a high level of learning in all content areas in their school or district. The AED study notes that NWP teachers make writing part of everything they do. Rather than treating writing as a separate subject, they see it as fundamental to teaching all subjects and integrate it across the curriculum. Strategies for writing across the curriculum in typical NWP classrooms included daily math journals in which students "explained concepts and reflected on what they had learned. They also wrote explanations of solutions to problems or compared and contrasted different mathematical concepts, such as quadrilaterals." Science journals were used for students to make a prediction, write observations and conclusions, or create an entry from a scientist's viewpoint. In social studies, students conducted family interviews and wrote biographies, news articles, and journals in the voice of real people or historical figures they were studying. These practices suggest that writing across the curriculum can be used in two ways: as a means to teach the student to master distinct forms and conventions of writing as practiced in diverse subjects areas (science reports, business plans, historical research, and so on) or as a means for the student to learn and retain content through more informal kinds of writing such as a journal or learning log.

The case study on expressive writing given here illustrates how writing in a content-specific area can be used to enhance learning.

CASE STUDY
Expressive Writing in a High School Biology Class

An important example of teacher research on writing in a content area dates from 1981, but it is still useful for understanding one aspect of learning that writing can support: retention of knowledge.

Robert Tierney, a biology teacher at Irvington High School in Fremont, California, believed that writing could be a powerful learning tool for his students. But for many of his colleagues, time spent writing was time lost for learning science. With so much content and knowledge to cover, students needed time to do science, not just read or write about it. Most of the writing done in science classes was functional or "transactional reporting": a lab write-up, a descriptive report, a multiple-choice test.

But Tierney, who is a Bay Area Writing Project teacher-consultant, believed there was also a place for what he terms "expressive writing": "Many biology teachers fail to realize its potential as a learning tool because they are not familiar with writing as a process. Few biology teachers are themselves writers. Yet modern biology instruction requires a hands-on, inquiry, think-through-the-problem approach. Expressive writing is a means of thinking through a problem. The student is free to do his [or her] thinking on paper without fear of the teacher as an examiner. Expressive writing can provide the biology student with essential experience of free inquiry—the essence of the scientific method."[10]

Expressive writing can take many forms, and Tierney suggests it is much like the language used in casual conversation or the writing that takes place in the "initial phase of thinking through a problem." He wanted to know what impact such writing could have on biology students. He decided to conduct a study to examine the question.

With his colleague, Harry Stookey, Tierney divided the 136 sophomore, junior, and senior biology students at Irvington into an experimental group and a comparison group. Both would cover the same topics at the same time, do the labs, and have homework assignments "corrected with a stress upon usage and spelling." Group one was designated "experimental," while group two served as the comparison. Although the students stayed with the same teacher for the year, each teacher gave distinct types of writing assignments after a semester, switching roles in directing the experimental and comparison groups, to negate the "teacher variable" in the experiment. The two groups were distinguished via their writing assignments:

Experimental Group	Comparison Group
1. Reading logs	1. No reading logs
2. Neuron notes or learning logs	2. No neuron notes
3. Practice essays	3. No practice essays
4. Writing to a specific audience other than the teacher	4. Writing to the teacher as an examiner
5. End-of-class summaries	5. No end-of-class summaries
6. Group writing	6. Limited group writing
7. Essay tests	7. Multiple-choice tests

To measure performance, two test units were selected, one on genetics in the first semester and one on seed plants in the second. For each, a pretest and posttest (using the same multiple-choice questions) were used, as well as recall tests (these were given sixteen weeks after the fall genetics unit and three weeks after the spring seed-plants unit). Although the results of the multiple-choice tests were about the same for each group, there were substantial differences in the recall test results: the experimental group scored noticeably higher than the comparison group. After sixteen weeks, the experimental group scored 11 percent higher on the genetics recall test; after three weeks, the same group scored 5 percent higher on the seed-comparison recall test. Tierney and Stookey concluded that the students who had the opportunity to use expressive writing retained more of what they learned. Further, they believe these students "learn the subject matter more thoroughly, and their papers, reflecting what the student actually understands, will be more interesting to read."[11] The study showed that expressive writing, a common writing-as-process strategy, helped improve student retention in a content-heavy science subject.

WRITING AS INQUIRY

Tierney's study is particularly relevant for middle and high school classrooms where knowledge becomes specialized and content is king. As George Hillocks notes, "Teaching writing has a venerable history of assuming that the demands of content will be taken care of elsewhere."[12] Tierney's study shows that expressive, informal writing tasks can improve learning retention. But learning content involves more than retention. Regardless of which content areas and specialties a teacher is responsible for, all teachers can use writing to help students reflect and think critically *about* content.

Hillocks argues that teachers must do more with writing than simply teach its forms and model its processes. They need to help students develop the basic inquiry strategies common to most disciplines and incorporate them in their writing activity. Such strategies lie at the core of the critical thinking that students must do in academia, in a profession, and as adult citizens in the real world beyond school. They include examining assumptions and prior knowledge, posing questions, making inferences and interpreting, establishing working hypotheses and testing interpretations, and, finally, imagining—which is perhaps the most powerful gateway of all, the foundation for original discovery and insight.

Teachers, writes Hillocks,[13] can encourage imagination through various applications of role playing: for developing an argument from diverse perspectives, for inventing a character and improvising action in various situations, for assuming the point of view of a literary character, and so on. He describes how Ellen Lewis, a writing specialist in Jefferson County, Kentucky, engages students in discovery and inquiry strategies by writing fiction. Lewis, says, Hillocks,

> developed a set of inquiry-based lessons for working on writing short stories. The sequence is based on a task analysis of what middle school students will have to know and be able to do in order to write a . . . short story. . . . The set of lessons takes students through finding story ideas, "mapping" them, "getting to know your characters, dividing the story into scenes, drafting the story, writing an effective lead . . . showing action, using dialogue to advance the plot, punctuating dialogue." Because the sequence begins with finding story ideas, all subsequent lessons can be tied to the writing of a short story. In fact many lessons call for use of materials that the students have created as they are progressing toward that goal. The important point is that the lessons engage students in the microprocesses of creating the details, dialogue, openings, and so forth that they will need to develop an effective story. These lessons do not simply employ general writing

Eventually someone got the bright idea to do things the way they are done in the third grade, and writing across the curriculum was reborn into high school and college curricula as though it were something brand new. Students can write about history, about geology, about sociology, about economics, about physics, about—heaven help us—mathematics. Even more to the point, students can explore concepts, make connections, conceive ideas through writing if every piece of writing isn't supposed to be formal, complete, and correct, a caricature of what is published in academic journals. Write to learn! Now, why hadn't someone thought of that before?

Jerry Herman, "*Writing to Learn,* by William Zinsser," p. 16.

processes; they recognize the need to provide much more detailed help by teaching students strategies that enable them to wrest appropriate support and elaboration from their content. One would hope that all writing teachers would begin to use this sort of thoughtful analysis of the writing tasks they teach.[14]

Professional Development

Today, many districts and principals are setting high standards and expectations for staff development. They demand models and activities that promote lasting change. They want professional development to offer research-based strategies whose effectiveness has been correlated with impact on teaching practice and student performance.

Effective professional development requires time and resources if it is to take root. It can involve a broad range of interventions and formats, tied to specific curricular aims, unfolding over a one-to-three-year cycle, with clearly defined short-term and long-term goals. Ample research from the last decade shows that staff development is both a crucial element in school reform and a catalyst for change in building a school culture that supports a high level of adult and student learning.[1] In a study for Stanford's Center for Research on the Context of Secondary Teaching, Milbrey McLaughlin and Joan Talbert conclude that "teachers' groups, professional communities variously defined, offer the most effective unit of intervention and powerful opportunity for reform." Such a network for educational change succeeds because it presents a "context for sustained learning and developing the profession." Systemic reform, they argue, "cannot be accomplished through traditional staff development models—episodic, decontextualized injections of 'knowledge' and technique. The path to change in the classroom core lies within and through teachers' professional communities; learning communities which generate knowledge, craft new

> Given the opportunity, teachers can and will make significant changes in their practices and perspectives on teaching and learning. And nowhere have these changes been more profound than in urban classrooms in which teachers are challenged by the demands of and differences among today's students.
>
> Ann Lieberman and Milbrey McLaughlin, "Networks for Educational Change," p. 677

norms of practice, and sustain participants in their efforts to reflect, examine, experiment, and change."[2]

A frequently cited example of successful districtwide school reform strategy is Community District 2 in New York City. It has been called "one of the highest performing urban school systems in the country with overall, fewer than 12 percent of its students . . . scoring in the lowest quartile of nationally standardized reading tests. A comparable figure for most urban districts is 40–50 percent."[3]

When Anthony Alvarado began his eight-year tenure as superintendent in 1987, this ethnically and economically diverse district (roughly 50 percent of its students come from a family officially designated as below the poverty line) ranked tenth in reading and fourth in mathematics out of thirty-two subdistricts. By 1996, it ranked second in both subjects.[4] Alvarado's approach emphasized professional development as the principal engine for effecting systemwide instructional improvement. As described by Richard Elmore in a 1997 report for the National Commission on Teaching and Learning, Alvarado's strategies for systemic change were built around seven organizing principles:

1. It's about instruction . . . and only about instruction.

2. Instructional change is a long, multi-stage process.

3. Shared expertise is the driver of instructional change.

4. Focus on system-wide improvement.

5. Good ideas come from talented people working together.

6. Set clear expectations, then decentralize.

7. Collegiality, caring, and respect.[5]

This chapter examines why staff development is needed for teaching writing and explores models and strategies for effective professional development such as those initiated by Alvarado in New York City. It describes what a successful model can do. It also explains the rationale for the National Writing Project's model of staff development: teachers teaching teachers.

WHY DO WE NEED PROFESSIONAL DEVELOPMENT IN WRITING?

Teachers' knowledge of the subjects they teach and access to the latest research and materials related to it are essential to achieving a high level of student performance, according to a recent set of standards published by the National Association of Elementary School Principals.[6] A 1996 National Commission on Teaching and America's Future report makes the case more directly: teacher expertise is the most significant factor in student success. It cites studies showing that teacher qualifications account for 40 percent of the difference in overall student performance and that teacher quality is more powerful than a student's socioeconomic background in student learning.[7]

Those findings raise a core question that touches on the teaching of writing and its role in improving student literacy. According to Sandra Gibbs of the National Council of Teachers of English, very few states require specific coursework in the teaching of writing for certification. A survey of state requirements conducted for this publication supports her view: Missouri, Delaware, and Idaho are the only states that specifically require such coursework for teacher licensing. On the brighter side, more and more public universities are offering courses in teaching writing. Most states, according to the National Association of State Directors of Teacher Education and Certification, now test potential teachers on their basic writing skills. Writing expertise is embedded in state competency requirements with varying degrees of rigor. Some requirements, like Vermont's, expect knowledge of the composing process as well as the ability to teach writing across genres. But in

> Schools need to be considered as places for teachers to lead scholarly lives. I can't imagine providing quality education for students if schools don't take the teaching of teachers seriously. . . . When teachers delight in their own professional discoveries, their students reap the rewards. How many times have educators asked, "Would you go to a doctor who doesn't keep up with the latest findings and techniques?"
>
> Shelley Harwayne, *Going Public,* p. 241

terms of coursework and competency requirements, the disparity between those for reading and those for writing is striking. Yet research shows that literacy is reading *and* writing and the two are best learned together.

Professional development in writing addresses a national need for improving teacher expertise not only in literacy and English language arts (ELA) but also for improving student performance in all areas of learning. Writing, as educators cited in this publication have stated, is complicated to teach because of the multifarious instructional needs of students in classrooms at all levels. Writing is not a "subject" that can be learned in a semester or a year, or even a decade, of a student's educational life, because the writing tasks students are asked to do change and expand in difficulty as they move through academia.

We cannot build a nation of educated people
who can communicate effectively without teachers
and administrators who value, understand,
and practice writing themselves.

The changing and diverse student population in the American classroom today is another reason teachers need to keep learning new techniques and instructional strategies. It is not just ELA teachers who need to learn them. As the role of writing in learning across the disciplines becomes more apparent, every teacher has a responsibility to incorporate it in his or her classroom. We cannot build a nation of educated people who can communicate effectively without teachers and administrators who value, understand, and practice writing themselves.

Finally, professional development in writing is needed because it takes time to build a successful writing program, as Donald H. Graves discovered in his study of twelve high-performing school districts in Maine (see Chapter Six). There are no overnight success stories.

In a 1994–95 study for Columbia University's Center for Restructuring Education, Schools, and Teaching, Linda Darling-Hammond compared the

> ## How Much Time and Money?
>
> The National Staff Developmental Council (NSDC) urges that at least
> 25 percent of teachers' time should be given over to improving their
> expertise and to collaboration with colleagues. Endorsing this figure,
> the National Association of Elementary School Principals also concurs
> with NSDC's recommendations that, ideally, 5–10 percent of the
> school budget should be allotted to professional development oppor-
> tunities for teachers and instructional staff (National Association of Ele-
> mentary School Principals, *Leading Learning Communities*, p. 42).

weekly time allotted to staff development in a typical, large New York City
high school and two smaller restructured high schools. In the restructured
schools, 6–7.5 hours per week were spent on joint planning and staff development time for teachers. In the large, traditional high school only forty-
five minutes were allotted to such activities each week.[8]

WHAT HAPPENS IN EFFECTIVE PROFESSIONAL DEVELOPMENT: THE CASE OF NEW YORK CITY'S DISTRICT 2

Professional development models and programs need to be tailored to the
specific needs of a school. As described in the 1997 Elmore report,[9] Alvarado
used a variety of models:

- *A professional development laboratory.* In this model, experienced prac-
titioners are selected by district staff in consultation with principals, school
directors, and the head of the lab. They in turn accept a limited number of
teachers as visitors to their classrooms. "Each visiting teacher," writes Elmore, "spends three weeks of intensive observation and supervised practice
in the resident teacher's classroom." Follow-up visits to consult on issues of
practice occur after a teacher completes the initial visiting cycle.
- *Instructional consulting services.* Consultants work directly with teachers and in groups in two arrangements, relying either on an outside consultant or on district personnel assigned to a particular instructional area.
Alvarado's first initiative focused on literacy, reading, and writing through

collaboration with Lucy Calkins at Teachers College, Columbia University. It evolved into a broad-scale involvement "to develop skills focused on the teaching of writing and the use of literature in the development of students' literacy." Elmore characterizes this model as "labor-intensive . . . in that it relies on extensive involvement by a consultant with individuals and small groups of teachers, repeatedly over time, around a limited set of instructional problems." It also implies "a long-term commitment to instructional improvement in a given content area" rather than constantly shifting priorities.

• *Intervisitation and peer networks.* This model is designed to bring teachers and principals into contact with exemplary practices. Developing a peer network through visits to other sites both within and outside the district served to strengthen teachers' sense of their professional community as well as their commitment to experiment with, reflect on, and change instructional practices.

• *Institute opportunities.* District 2 invested heavily in intensive training during and after the school year. A familiar model for staff development, its 1995 summer institutes included training in three levels of mathematics for elementary teachers, sessions on standards implementation, literacy institutes for middle school teachers, and an advanced literacy institute for experienced teachers. What distinguished their approach to such off-site training was the follow-up. "Summer institutes," said one district 2 administrator, "don't make any sense unless you have the resources to support direct assistance to teachers during the school year." Extensive changes in teacher practice must also have support in the classroom and from the school. The district considers its model of off-site training "a continuous investment in a few strands of content-focused training over a long term, designed to have a cumulative impact on teachers within the district."

Professional development can be school-based and homegrown. It can take place in the context of staff meetings and weekend retreats focused on studying specific strategies and topics, or in study groups built around surveying current writing and literacy research. These formats, however, should be an integral part of a school's ongoing staff development plan and serve the larger goal of building an ongoing culture of instructional innovation in the school. Shelley Harwayne, who served as a principal under Alvarado in New York City's District 2 and is now its superintendent, suggests activities such as those in the following list, centered on reading and writing instruction, as ongoing "study techniques" for weekly staff meetings.

- Reading and responding to related professional material
- Watching videotapes of fellow teachers at work
- Bringing students to a staff meeting and conferring with them publicly
- Presenting the results of colleagues' visits to one another's room or combining classes to co-teach a writing workshop
- Telling the story of a writer and his or her work and teasing out the implications for students
- Brainstorming new teaching techniques, volunteering to try them out, and sharing the results
- Looking at one piece of student work prepared on an overhead projector and imagining how a conference with the student would go
- Reading aloud children's literature and discussing how best to share it with students
- Crafting a minilesson and rehearsing its presentation with colleagues
- Visiting other schools, attending conferences or workshops, and sharing observations and notes
- Inviting guest speakers with expertise in a selected area of study
- Inviting adults to work on their own writing in order to closely understand techniques to be taught to children
- Collaborating on teaching plans for a new course of study
- Presenting a new course of study, workshop tool, or classroom ritual to get feedback from colleagues[10]

Classroom teachers took turns showing student work on the overhead projector. At each meeting two classroom teachers, one from an upper-grade class and one from a lower-grade class, would give the context for a piece of writing and then the teachers gathered would discuss the strengths of the piece. We would then, based on the history of the child provided by the teacher, suggest possible ways to confer with the child in order to lift the quality of the writing. At our next gathering, the classroom teacher would report on how she chose to work with the student and upon the effectiveness of her work.

Shelley Harwayne,
Writing Through Childhood, p. 240,
on a staff study group
at Manhattan New School

THE NWP: TEACHERS TEACHING TEACHERS

Since its founding in 1974, the National Writing Project (NWP) has focused on improving writing and learning in our nation's schools, putting teacher expertise and networks at the heart of its professional development model. A distinctive feature of its approach to instructional improvement has been to address the issue of aligning the K–12 and postsecondary worlds of educators. To date, its summer institutes are one of the only places where teachers, administrators, and university academics join as peers to develop themselves as writers and writing teachers. As Katherine Nolan, an education researcher and executive director of Project Align, observes, "Colleges have rarely defined what students need to know and be able to do in order to be successful writers. Nor have teacher prep programs or schools and districts articulated what they want new teachers to be able to do with writing. The NWP may be the only place where these various disconnects and problems of vagueness can be addressed" (letter to the author, January 9, 2002).

A distinctive feature of the NWP's approach to instructional improvement has been to address the issue of aligning the K–12 and postsecondary worlds of educators.

The National Writing Project is a professional network that presently links 175 college-based sites in fifty states, Washington, D.C., Puerto Rico, and the U.S. Virgin Islands. The NWP sponsored more than fifty-five hundred professional development programs in 2001 through its sites, including three thousand in-service workshops for teachers, more than a third of them part of ongoing partnerships with schools. One reason NWP workshops have been so popular with teachers is that they are led by highly skilled, experienced teachers. Most principals understand that teachers have good reason to be suspicious of the expertise of an outside professional consultant who may not have been near a classroom in years. As NWP founder James Gray says, "We believed that if school reform was to be effective, in-service programs must be conducted by the folks on the ground."[11]

In a recent study of two NWP sites, Ann Lieberman, a senior scholar at the Carnegie Foundation for the Advancement of Teaching, and Diane R. Wood, assistant professor at the University of Southern Maine, identified two key features of the NWP's approach to teacher development: "a distinctive set of *social practices* that motivate teachers, make learning accessible, and build an ongoing professional community; and *networks* that organize and sustain relationships among these communities and produce new and revitalizing forms of support, commitment, and leadership."[12]

The NWP believes that teachers are professionals who have knowledge to share. When principals visit or participate in a writing project staff development program, they should not expect to find a room of passive observers. A presenter who, because of her exemplary practice in the teaching of writing, has been invited to participate in a local NWP site's summer institute will be demonstrating a successful practice to fellow teachers. Teachers will be involved in hands-on testing of this practice, but as professionals with expertise of their own they are also encouraged to present what they know to the group.

One form of participation above all others is expected at NWP staff development: writing teachers must write. This expectation grounds NWP in-service in the actual practice of writing. Teachers are doing what they require their students to do; as described in Chapter Six, effective writing programs are built by teachers who write. James Gray quotes a typical comment from a summer institute participant: "I always thought I knew what revision meant until this summer. Now I know what revision means."[13]

The NWP's professional development model is one that has demonstrably improved writing education in the schools (see the AED study

> Because literacy lies at the heart of school achievement and extends to every subject area, writing project sites reach whole schools. Because we promote teacher-conducted professional development, and practitioner research, we develop leadership. Because we provide summer institute experiences that are often transforming, we understand change.
>
> Joe Check, associate professor, Graduate College of Education, University of Massachusetts, and director of the Boston Writing Project

Studies showing the NWP's impact on student performance and behavior are numerous. Often using a controlled comparative method, studies have demonstrated that the NWP leads to increases in student achievement. . . . The NWP provides efficient and effective staff development to teachers who wish to improve their students' performance in writing. As a long-standing program with rigorous, ongoing evaluation, the NWP is a model of teacher-driven, focused staff development that can be altered to accommodate the specific needs of schools and districts.

Joellen Killion, *What Works in the Middle: Results-Based Staff Development*, p. 52

described in Chapter Three, and the NWP publication *Profiles of the National Writing Project*).[14] But as many principals have learned the hard way, staff development that improves practice is not accomplished in a single afternoon. The NWP understands that if writing teachers are to learn effectively from their colleagues, they need to participate in an in-depth program, one that allows them to try out in their classrooms what they learn from one another and to share what they find out.

The NWP model urges multiple sessions coordinated by a teacher-consultant who determines the specific needs of the group and finds colleagues who can lead sessions that help teachers address their expressed concerns. This focused and extended concentration on best practice in the teaching of writing has an added benefit. As a result of involvement with NWP programs, teachers often become teacher-researchers who examine in-depth what is going on in their own writing classrooms. Principals find that knowledge gained and shared in this way can greatly advance the faculty knowledge base for teaching practice. The NWP has served as a strong advocate for teacher research.

But if the NWP in-service model, with its emphasis on voluntary participation, teacher expertise, extended programs, and teacher research, is to work, then another key ingredient must be added to the mix: a committed administrator. To commit to the concept that classroom teachers are the linchpin of all school reform, including the improved teaching and learning of writing, is crucial to success. As Jim Gray has written, "school reform can't happen just by passing laws and publishing mandates. But real school reform can happen when teachers come together regularly throughout their careers to explore practices that effective teachers have already proven are successful in their classrooms."[15]

CASE STUDY
A Scenario for Change

In an article for the NWP's Quarterly,[16] *Joe Check, director of the Boston Writing Project (BWP), described how he used a reflective writing technique in a professional development workshop to open up new areas of awareness for faculty about the troublesome problem of diverse literacies.*

Several years ago, a BWP teacher-consultant asked me to work with her during the opening sessions of a year-long professional development series. The Boston elementary school we were working with had low test scores, high enrollment, and a student body that was highly diverse, including a majority of African American students and bilingual programs in both Spanish and Haitian Creole. At the second after-school workshop, which included the whole faculty and principal, we asked participants to do a piece of short, memory-based personal writing—a standard technique both of us had used many times before. This time, we added a single sentence to the directions: "Please feel free to write in whatever language you feel most comfortable."

Immediately, the dynamics in the room changed. When it came time to share aloud, we encouraged those who had not written in English to read what they had written just as they had written it, and then to provide an impromptu English translation.

The discussion that followed was rich and animated, and opened up in an unprecedented way major issues of language status, "correctness," pedagogy, and philosophy that

> The most reliable and credible solutions to the problems of learning and teaching that face classroom teachers and their students are to be found in the reservoir of wisdom and practical knowledge . . . of successful classroom teachers themselves. Thus the writing project looks to experienced and successful classroom teachers as the best resource available to the educational community for solving the academic problems that trouble us. Teachers are . . . not seen as the source of the problem but as the principal resource for the solution.
>
> Sheridan Blau, "The Only Thing New Under the Sun: Twenty-Five Years of the National Writing Project," p. 2

The local networks of Writing Project sites encourage posing problems and asking questions rather than providing prescriptive or prepackaged answers, offering teachers opportunities to respond to the particular needs of their urban, rural, or suburban contexts. Involved in creating and implementing these activities, teachers develop an appreciation of the continual challenges of teaching and a sophisticated notion of what it means to be a professional teacher capable of responding to the needs of diverse students in a changing world.

Ann Lieberman and Diane Wood,
"The National Writing Project," p. 43

had been boiling just under the surface. Some of the bilingual teachers said that they had never before felt free to express themselves as professionals in their first language and that it was a liberating experience. Others, both bilingual and regular education teachers, wondered if we were sending the wrong message, devaluing the importance of English, which was, after all, the key to school success for both bilingual and monolingual children. Some teachers pointed out that the situation of those African American children who spoke nonstandard English at home was in some ways similar to the situation of the Spanish and Haitian-speaking children. Among several of the Haitian teachers, there was conflict over whether their "real" first language was Haitian Creole, an emerging language, or the traditional French in which much Haitian schooling is conducted.

At the end of the time period, few wanted to leave. It had become clear to all that beliefs revealed in this conversation were affecting teaching and learning in the school in an important, hitherto hidden way.

The read-aloud in three languages was a breakthrough moment for that workshop series; it acted like a lightning bolt suddenly illuminating the true tension and complexity inherent in literacy learning in the school. After that moment neither teachers nor workshop leaders pretended that better reading and writing could be achieved simply by applying an appropriate selection of "best practices." Something far deeper and more personal was at stake. By June, the school had made substantial progress in defining for itself its own shared philosophy of writing, based on those things the whole staff could agree on, and individual teachers and clusters of teachers had shared and learned new techniques, analyzed student work and their own teaching, and made significant change in their classroom approaches to literacy.

The philosophy statement, when viewed from the outside, contained little that was surprising: writing was a process, writing should be done regularly and in a variety of forms at all grade levels, there were many different "correct" techniques for teaching writing, parents should be regularly informed both of writing lessons and why the lessons were designed as they were, improved literacy in the first language strengthened English language learning, all the school's students had the right to regular instruction in English fluency and usage. Its importance was that it embodied a set of negotiations around differing and strongly held beliefs that had started the teachers and principal on the road to schoolwide change—to becoming not a replication of a national exemplar, but their own "exemplary context."

Standards and Assessments for Writing

State curriculum documents and assessments are carrying a new message: writing should no longer be "the silent R" of learning, or the poor cousin of reading. The standards movement has helped to focus attention on writing in all disciplines and to push for consistency within standards, assessment, and rubrics.[1] In many states, improving student writing and setting higher standards for it across the grades have become important goals of school reform. A work in progress, this trend in curriculum reform efforts reverses decades of inattention to the centrality of writing in the learning process.

State curriculum documents and assessments are now carrying a new message: writing should no longer be "the silent R" of learning. The standards movement has helped to focus attention on writing in all disciplines.

This chapter looks at common elements underlying standards for writing and how writing is reflected in standards for other disciplines as well. It suggests some principles for assessing student writing and presents case studies of how assessment can be used effectively to understand student progress and instructional needs.

A NATION OF WRITERS?

A recent New Jersey performance standard for writing states that "all students will write in clear, concise, organized language that varies in content and form for different audiences and purposes."[2] Kentucky sets a similar goal for portfolio assessment of writing in grades four, seven, and twelve: "Promote each student's ability to communicate to a variety of audiences for a variety of purposes." On Illinois math assessments, students must write extended-response descriptions of their problem solving. A Michigan writing assessment asks students to "decide the genre and approach to fulfill a writing task," while its state content standards require students to "demonstrate understanding of issues and problems by making connections and generating themes within and across texts." These benchmarks correlate with national standards created by the International Reading Association and the National Council of Teachers of English (NCTE), such as the NCTE's call for students to "adjust their use of . . . language . . . to communicate effectively and for different purposes."[3]

Improving writing is now seen as important for learning subjects other than English. It is striking how other disciplines have begun to incorporate research on the composition process into their own teaching strategies. In 1986, the National Council of Teachers of Mathematics (NCTM) created a set of teaching and learning standards to improve the quality of K–12 instruction. "The standards," as they have come to be known, are recognized for their exceptional quality and have been endorsed by fifteen major scholarly societies, with support from thirty others. The process of their development has been widely credited as a means for effecting "systemic change in the teaching of a discipline."[4] Writing plays a crucial role in the NCTM standards for both middle and high school. As standard number two for grades nine through twelve states:

*Improving writing is now seen as important
for learning subjects other than English.*

Techniques used to teach writing can be useful in teaching mathematical communication. The view of writing as a process emphasizes brainstorming, clarifying, and revising; this view can readily be applied to solving a mathematical problem. The simple exercise of writing an explanation of how a problem was solved not only helps clarify a student's thinking but also may provide other students fresh insights gained from viewing the problem from a new perspective. Students should be encouraged to keep journals describing their mathematical experiences, including their reflections on their problem-solving processes. Journal writing also can help students clarify feelings about mathematics or about a particular experience or activity in a mathematics classroom.[5]

Clearly, this standard recognizes both the value of writing as problem solving and its expressive potential for students in a content-driven discipline. It supports what Robert Tierney (see the case study in Chapter Three) found about the use of expressive writing in biology as a tool for learning. It echoes what George Hillocks, Jr., has argued in *Teaching Writing as a Reflective Practice* about using writing to help the student learn inquiry strategies for discovering, elaborating, and testing ideas; he cites a 1987 report from the English Coalition Conference, *English for the Nineties and Beyond:* "Students must 'learn to be inquirers, experimenters, and problem solvers' . . . not only to become more effective writers and readers but to become more fully participating citizens in a rapidly changing world."[6]

IMPLEMENTING STANDARDS

As of 2000, forty-nine states have established some academic standards for their schools. Debate over quality continues: Are state standards too high, or too low? How they will affect teaching and learning? Creating high standards alone is not sufficient to improve learning in schools; it is the teacher who makes them come alive in the classroom. Successful implementation requires that the teacher know how to translate standards through classroom practice that supports a high level of learning. But many teachers feel they do not. For example, the National Assessment of Title I found that "in 1998 only 37 percent of teachers in [Title I] schools reported that they felt very well prepared to implement state or district curriculum and performance standards."[7]

A crucial need, then, is professional development for all teachers (see Chapter Four). The situation is particularly acute in light of a teacher shortage and high turnover. According to U.S. Department of Education figures, in 1998 more than two-thirds (70 percent) of teachers in high-poverty schools received fewer than nine hours per year of professional development related to content and performance standards. Administrators can play a substantial role by providing resources and professional development that help teachers get standards off the page and into the classroom. Professional development that gives teachers resources and exposure to best classroom practices, as well as time to think through how high standards are best implemented, is a crucial element in making standards more than a well-intentioned piece of paper. The principal has an essential role in providing resources and leadership for sustaining a vision of shared expectations for high learning.

Unfortunately, what we have in too many districts . . . is test-driven reform masquerading as standards-based reform.

Warren Simmons, quoted in Lynn Olson, "Worries of a Standards 'Backlash' Grow"

However, in some states, according to professor of education and sociology Anthony S. Byrk,[8] the real "load-bearing wall" for instruction may be assessments rather than standards documents. For many educators, there is concern that "teaching, standards, and tests are not aligned."[9] Standards may promise a rich curriculum, but if assessments are only loosely tied to the learning objectives of standards and frameworks, they may undermine or weaken effective teaching practices.

State assessments are changing, but schools can still exercise control by developing quality writing programs. The classroom is where the real assessment of learning happens. "Teachers," argues Hillocks, "have always known that writing is the means of assessing high levels of conceptualizing, analysis, application, synthesis, and argument. Good essay exams do not call for simple regurgitation of material memorized from a text or the teacher's lectures, but require the synthesis of material drawn directly from many sources in ways that may not have been dealt with directly in class, in ways that reveal true understanding."[10]

THE IMPACT OF WRITING ASSESSMENTS ON THE CLASSROOM

How closely are state writing assessments aligned with standards, and how do they affect the teaching of writing? A recent study by Hillocks, who received an NCTE award for distinguished research, looked at writing assessments in five states: Illinois, Kentucky, New York, Oregon, and Texas.[11] The states were selected for differences in assessment type, the stakes of the testing, and their geography. In each state, Hillocks interviewed policymakers, administrators, and teachers in six school districts from diverse settings. When he began his study, thirty-seven of the fifty states had some form of writing assessment; his study presents the most in-depth look to date both at the quality of state assessments and their impact on teaching methods.

Hillocks found that writing assessments vary widely from state to state. Variables include the type of writing assessed, the nature of the prompts used as well as their number and variety, the stakes (for school and student), how the assessments are administered (time allotted, scoring personnel, and so on), and the rubrics or criteria for judging student work. For example, Kentucky and Oregon require both on-demand and portfolio assessments. Other states call for on-demand writing only. "While Kentucky students have a school year . . . to produce their writing for assessment, Illinois students have only forty minutes, and Texas students have a school day."[12] New York emphasizes expository

As we consider the issues of standards and assessments, we need to consider what kind of accountability is genuine accountability, and what kind of strategies, in fact, enhance teaching and learning.

Linda Darling-Hammond, "Making Relationships Between Standards, Frameworks, Assessment, Evaluation, Instruction, and Accountability," p. 2

writing. Oregon evaluates imaginative, expository, narrative, and persuasive writing. In Kentucky and New York, teachers in the building score the writing; in Illinois and Texas, the tests go to a private company. New York and Texas require the student to pass the test to graduate; in Illinois, how students fare has no impact on their academic progress. Low scores in Texas may result in a school district being placed under supervision, or even dismantled. The merits or liabilities of these differences are open to question, but they do, as Hillocks found, have a profound impact on how teachers prepare students for assessment.

Much of his study focuses on the disparity between assessment rubrics or criteria and the standards they are meant to reflect. Hillocks argues that in certain states the rubrics are vague and the kind of instruction they promote is of low quality and little use to students. He cites as examples instruction that relies on formulaic writing (the five-paragraph essay) and assessment prompts that ask students to write quickly on random topics without offering data or information. Such practices "engender vacuous writing," set low standards for teaching writing, and eliminate "the need for critical thought. It [the five-paragraph theme] teaches students that any reasons they propose in support of a proposition need not be examined for consistency, evidentiary force, or even relevance."[13]

Decades of research have also shown that, however expedient and economical skills drills may be, they fail over the long run to improve student writing, much less to assess a student's developmental needs.[14] As Freedman and Daiute observe: "Writing assessments . . . do not always acknowledge issues of culture, process, or purpose. When such tests carry high stakes, they can dominate classroom life in ways that diminish opportunities, for example, by forcing teachers to spend inordinate amounts of time drilling students on grammatical rules out of context, something that has not been found to support writing development."[15]

School administrators and teachers can support student growth and improvement in writing with clear goals for assessing student work. Whatever assessment instruments are used for writing, there must be an explicit connection among curricular aims, standards, instructional needs, the test, and its scoring criteria or rubrics. For teachers and students, assessment should have an *instructional* purpose, not simply an evaluative or administrative one. That is, it should identify and diagnose a specific problem in student writing or adjust a lesson plan to meet student needs as they are uncovered. To know how well students are doing, teachers and administrators should use or consider (1) extended writing samples; (2) writing in multiple genres; (3) valid rubrics; (4) writing over time, across genres and content areas; and (5) student participation in developing assessment.

For teachers and students, assessment should have an instructional *purpose, not simply an evaluative or administrative one.*

Extended Writing Samples

Short-answer and multiple-choice tests can be useful for assessing certain kinds of knowledge in content areas, but they reveal little about the breadth of student writing ability or instructional needs. Provided that valid rubrics and benchmarks are linked to explicit standards for them, extended writing samples can give a teacher a clearer picture of a student's ability with tasks such as the following:

- Organizing information
- Generating and developing ideas
- Constructing a convincing and nuanced argument
- Creating a coherent story line

A longer writing sample also gives a more complete picture of a student's understanding of the mechanics and conventions of grammar, punctuation, and spelling.

Writing in Multiple Genres

Single-prompt writing assessments may be useful as a snapshot of student achievement (or for evaluating the effectiveness of a writing program), but because they focus on a single type or genre of writing

Many state writing assessments run the risk of undercutting good writing by scoring only for focus, organization, style, and mechanics without once asking judges to consider whether the writing is powerful, memorable, provocative, or moving (all impact-related criteria, and all at the heart of why people read what others write).

Grant Wiggins,
Educative Assessment, p. 67

(argument, description, and the like) they have limited value for understanding a writer's overall strengths or weaknesses. A student may be able to summarize a movie plot but lack experience with more sophisticated tasks of "critical literacy" such as assessing divergent viewpoints and framing or dissecting arguments—the standard fare of academic writing at the university level. The student may be gifted in self-expression and first-person writing but lack experience with or understanding of the conventions of various kinds of expository prose.

"As a teacher," writes Sandra Murphy, a professor at the University of California, Davis, "I have long since learned to be suspicious of any attempt to judge student writers on the basis of a single piece of writing collected on a single occasion. Experience has taught me, and research has confirmed, that it may not be possible to take a student's performance on a single occasion and use it to predict what will happen on others, in other contexts, in other genres."[16] Multiple samples of student work, each written for a distinct audience and purpose, can give a much deeper sense of a writer's abilities and developmental needs.

Valid Rubrics

Rubrics should focus on appropriate criteria for the task assessed. "Validity," argues Grant Wiggins, "is a matter of determining what is permissible to infer from scores."[17] He gives the example of an assessment in narrative writing that exclusively emphasizes spelling and grammar. The scoring might be reliable quantitatively "because it is easy to count such errors . . . [but] they would yield invalid inferences about students' ability to write stories effectively."[18] Spelling accuracy, he adds, does not correlate with writing an engaging story, which is the student's task; even though the rubric would be measuring a particular writing trait accurately, it is not in line with what the assessment sets out to measure. Hillocks's study of state writing assessments finds this to be a common assessment flaw. Rubrics for such traits as how well ideas are developed or how well evidence is used in persuasive writing are ambiguous, or they are simply quantitative—for example, the number of supports for a claim is considered but not their quality or accuracy.[19]

Writing over Time, Across Genres and Content Areas

Assessment can measure development and growth over time by looking at a collection of writing, such as a portfolio or writing folder. Looking at a body of work can yield more data about student progress and a richer diagnostic for the teacher. For the student, this approach creates an opportunity to be more actively engaged in the assessment process. For the teacher, it can be a springboard for reshaping strategies and planning new classroom activities geared to the specific needs of the individual student.

> *For the student, using a portfolio creates an opportunity to be more actively engaged in the assessment process. For the teacher, it can be a springboard for reshaping strategies and planning new classroom activities geared to the specific needs of the individual student.*

A portfolio is any kind of folder or binder that students keep to showcase their written work. Its use varies widely in the classroom. Although a portfolio can serve all three of the assessment purposes described earlier, proponents see its main strength as instructional. A portfolio often includes multiple drafts and samples of various genres of writing completed over the course of a semester or year. It can also collect writing from diverse subject areas. Used strategically, a portfolio can give the teacher a powerful developmental picture of how a student is progressing. It offers a much richer picture of a student's writing than a single writing-on-demand assessment can, particularly one administered in a short time frame that precludes student revision.

BETTY JANE WAGNER
Portfolio Assessment

Betty Jane Wagner is a professor in the Reading and Language Department at National-Louis University and coauthor with James Moffett of the influential Student-Centered Language Arts, K–12, *now in its fourth edition. As former director of the Chicago Area Writing Project and former chair of the NCTE's Language and Learning Across the Curriculum Committee, she is a strong advocate of writing portfolios.*

Student ownership is key. The best practice is a portfolio where a student's best writing determines the grade for the term. I try to encourage people to have the students select their best work, and that is what gets evaluated. That's the way professional writers work—the last draft I had time for is what gets published. I try to get as many people to look at it as possible. And that's how kids should begin to feel about their writing. It's the student ownership that will make that happen, and then it doesn't much matter what the teacher does, as long as she stays in the coaching role.

CASE STUDY
Assessing Writing Growth in a Bilingual Elementary School

Each year, at La Escuela Fratney, a K–5 two-way bilingual (Spanish and English) Milwaukee public school, student work is presented at an end-of-the-year exhibition. It is the culmination of the school's student-centered, "structured project" approach to learning. Bob Petersen, winner of Wisconsin's 1995 Elementary Teacher of the Year award and a founding editor of *Rethinking Schools,* explains the approach:

"Throughout the year, fifth-grade students are expected to

complete major projects. These projects include a student autobiography, a report in Spanish on an endangered animal, a bilingual poetry anthology, a report on a famous person who fought for social justice, and a self-reflection report on the student's journey through elementary school."

Petersen added the exhibition component after seeing a display of student portfolios at a New York City high school. He found it an effective way to motivate both teachers and students. At the start of each year, Petersen tells his students that the exhibition will be held in the school's gymnasium and that it will first be viewed by third and fourth graders to prepare them for their next year's work. Then the exhibit will be opened to parents and the community at large, including university people, school board members, local business leaders, school staff, and others.

The exhibit represents students' learning for their entire school career, including alphabet books and stories from kindergarten and first grade; math projects involving student surveys of classmates' TV viewing habits, ethnic background, and favorite football players (the surveys used circle graphs, percentages, and fractions); and their written projects. Petersen continues to refine the exhibit. He now sets requirements at the beginning of the year, creating performance rubrics and evaluation guides with the students to ensure higher quality work on their major projects. A self-reflection component has also been added. It asks students to "step back and think about what they've learned and how they might improve on similar projects in the future." Students also create bilingual scripts that they practice with a partner as a means for preparing what they say at the exhibit about their overall learning. Such practices emphasize both metacognitive skills and student ownership of their work.

I figured such a public exhibition of work would help motivation. It would also help me maintain high expectations for my students. If teachers know that their students are going to present their work so publicly, they're less likely to while away the days assigning meaningless worksheets. Their curriculum will be more oriented to projects and the real world. This is a good example of the idea that if the "test" is a good one, it's fine to have it drive the curriculum.

Bob Petersen, "Motivating Students to Do Quality Work," p. 1

Student Participation in Developing Assessment

Bob Petersen's portfolio exhibition is striking for how his students share responsibility for assessment and highlights the importance of student ownership of their work. Not only are they involved in creating rubrics for their own work, but they have the opportunity to reflect on their growth as learners. Many writing teachers have found that engaging students as active participants in the assessment process is an effective classroom practice: it enables them to assume more responsibility for their learning and brings clarity to what often appear to students as arbitrary or inconsistent standards about good writing. Peer response can be another effective means for participation and engagement, so long as students are given the necessary skills and knowledge to respond critically to one another's work. Peer response helps students take responsibility for the quality of the work and can support a climate for high standards and expectations in writing.

To develop as writers, students also need the opportunity to articulate their own awareness and understanding of their processes in learning to write. Research[20] has shown the importance of such metacognitive thinking in becoming a better writer. Self-assessment of strengths and weaknesses, strategies used to improve writing, and their progress and goals for writing can be used by students to demonstrate their learning. Providing such information should be an integral component of writing assessment, as suggested in such guides as the New Standards Project's *Student Portfolio Handbook: Middle School English Language Arts.*[21] Just as students are asked for a written description of how they solved a math problem in some classrooms and in state assessments, so should they be asked periodically to reflect on their writing strategies as well as their goals and progress. Such writing tasks are an excellent opportunity for students to apply inquiry and critical thinking to themselves and their identities as learners.

To develop as writers, students all need the opportunity to articulate their own awareness of their processes in learning to write.

CASE STUDY
Assessment in Kentucky

For the past ten years, Kentucky has made a serious commitment to improving student writing. But prior to 1990, says Starr Lewis, assistant commissioner of Kentucky's Department of Education, "students did precious little writing in [the state's] schools" and most of it involved the expedient five-paragraph theme.[22] Today, its portfolio development guidelines discourage such formulaic writing. Instead, they stress student ownership and quality writing instruction anchored in the writing process. Kentucky uses both writing-on-demand and portfolio assessment in grades four, seven, and twelve. It defines portfolio assessment as "purposeful selection of student work that exhibits a student's efforts and achievements." As outlined in its 1999 Teacher Handbook, the goals of writing portfolio assessment are to

- Provide students with skills, knowledge, and confidence necessary to become independent thinkers and writers
- Promote each student's ability to communicate to a variety of audiences for a variety of purposes
- Document student performance on various kinds of writing that have been developed over time
- Integrate performance with classroom instruction
- Provide information upon which to base ongoing development of a curriculum that is responsive to student needs

At the high school senior level, Kentucky's writing portfolio assessment requires five pieces of writing and a letter to reviewers reflecting on the writer's own work and development. The other pieces include one personal-expressive, one imaginative, and three transactional pieces (writing to persuade or to inform). Of these five, two must come from subjects other than English.

Kentucky Holistic Scoring Guide

Novice

- Limited awareness of audience or purpose

- Minimal idea development; limited or unrelated details

- Random or weak organization

- Incorrect or ineffective sentence structure

- Incorrect or ineffective language

- Errors in spelling, punctuation, and capitalization are disproportionate to length and complexity

Apprentice

- Some evidence of communicating with an audience for a specific purpose; some lapses in focus

- Unelaborated idea development; unelaborated or repetitious details

- Lapses in organization or coherence

- Simplistic or awkward sentence structure

- Simplistic or imprecise language

- Some errors in spelling, punctuation, and capitalization that do not interfere with communication

Proficient

- Focused on a purpose; communicates with an audience; evidence of voice and suitable tone

- Depth of idea development supported by elaborated, relevant details

- Logical, coherent organization

- Controlled and varied sentence structure

- Acceptable, effective language

- Few errors in spelling, punctuation, and capitalization relative to length and complexity

Distinguished

- Establishes a purpose and maintains clear focus; strong awareness of audience; evidence of distinctive voice and appropriate tone

- Depth and complexity of ideas supported by rich, engaging, and pertinent details; evidence of analysis, reflection, insight

- Careful and subtle organization

- Variety in sentence structure and length enhances effect

- Precise and rich language

- Control of spelling, punctuation, and capitalization

In his study of state writing assessments, George Hillocks gives the Kentucky assessment system high marks. "Clearly," he writes, "the spectrum of writing used in the Kentucky assessment is far broader than in any other state examined in detail in this study and broader than that in any of the other states with writing assessments."[23] Beyond the rich array of writing samples, "it provides . . . time for students to develop pieces of writing adequately so that they do not have to revert to the formulaic."[24] It also had the highest percentage of support from teachers in any state surveyed. "Over three quarters (76.6 percent)," Hillocks writes, "believe that the state assessment supports the kind of writing programs they would want in their schools. Over two thirds (67.2 percent) are positive about the scoring rubric. . . . But perhaps the most impressive is that nearly 80 percent of the teachers interviewed feel that the portfolio assessment has helped improve writing in the state. No other state writing assessment studied comes close to having such a strong endorsement for its appropriateness and its power in bringing about change."[25] Kentucky also ranked third in the nation in *Education Week*'s 2002 evaluations of each state's performance on standards and accountability in all core subjects.[26]

What Administrators Can Do to Create Effective Writing Programs

This book has examined the challenge of improving student writing in the light of new research in the field of composition, the changing needs of schools, successful classroom practices that mirror the work of writers in the real world, and how learning to write is also a matter of writing to learn. But what is the administrator's role in building an effective writing program? What practical steps can an administrator take to meet this crucial challenge for educational reform?

A critical component in building an effective writing program is an administrative philosophy that understands the power of writing as a tool for achieving high levels of learning and expression across all grades and content areas. As instructional leaders, school administrators responsible for implementing curriculum reform can play a vital role in devising and advocating for effective writing programs. This chapter describes how some principals and superintendents have worked with teachers to meet the challenge of creating a writing program that improves performance and builds confidence and capability for the student writer. It explores the strategies and ingredients of success. It tells the story of Sheldon Berman, a district superintendent in Hudson, Massachusetts, who used writing across the curriculum to help transform a "quietly underperforming high school" into an award-winning model of education reform. It also describes how writing across the curriculum was successfully used in an unlikely setting: a New York City high school established for recent immigrants with very limited English proficiency.

STRATEGIES FOR EFFECTIVE WRITING PROGRAMS

Writing researchers, curriculum coordinators, superintendents, principals, and teachers whom we interviewed identified a number of essential strategies for creating and sustaining a successful writing program:

Provide Vision and Leadership

Administrators are key players in promoting writing programs and meaningful writing standards in their schools. They impart strategic instructional leadership by working with their faculty to

- Devise long-term plans for improving writing and communicating them to the entire school community

- Craft policy statements addressed to staff and parents that articulate a rationale for why writing matters and why improving it should be a focus of the entire school community

- Assess the status of writing and of teaching it in the individual school

- Enlist teacher leaders as advocates for improving the teaching of writing in all classrooms

- Commit time and provide the necessary resources, such as professional development, research materials, and workshops for teachers to develop as writers and learn about research-proven classroom strategies

- Build creative administrative structures that support change and have broad support and buy-in from the school community

- Find practical solutions to such problems as scheduling and funding

How One Principal Got Teachers to Focus on Writing

When Rob Alpert, now director of instructional services in the San Ramon Valley Unified School District of Danville, California, was a principal, teachers knew it was a good idea to bring a pen and paper to faculty meetings. That's because, following his involvement in the Bay Area Writing Project at the University of California, Berkeley, Alpert decided he would devote a portion of some faculty meetings to having teachers write.

"It really wasn't my purpose to model," says Alpert. "I just wanted teachers to share and talk about their lives. We had teachers who had been working in rooms next to each other for twenty years and knew absolutely nothing about each other. I had some prompts I'd picked up from the writing project that worked well: a house they'd once lived in, their names, stuff about their kids and families."

Alpert says the teachers got used to writing together. "We'd talk about how it was different to write something than to just say it. And we were regularly reminded of what it is that we ask students to do when we require them to write. I never said 'Now take this back and try it in your classroom,' but later, when we looked at student work, we were in a much better position to develop standards for assessment because we had been writers ourselves."

Conduct a Districtwide or Schoolwide Writing Survey

Collecting samples of student writing and teachers' assignments within and across grade levels generates indispensable data for assessing the state of writing in a given district or school and for focusing attention on specific curricular needs. Samples of distinct genres and types of writing (narrative, persuasive, analytical, personal, and so on) from diverse subject areas should be discussed and evaluated by faculty to help identify standards and common expectations. A survey of staff and students can be used to understand attitudes toward writing and to establish common standards.

A survey of the state of writing in a school or district can lay the groundwork for a collective vision of what needs to be changed. The survey should address such questions as the following:

- Who is actually teaching writing?

- How many faculty and staff members enjoy writing and spend time doing it?

- How much and what kind of writing is done in the classroom? outside the classroom? (See the box "A Checklist for Administrators.")

- Do teachers and staff have consistent expectations for good writing?

- Do teachers share a common understanding of how students develop as writers and how writing can be a tool for learning in all disciplines?

- Do students have the opportunity to choose what they write about?

- How many hours per week are devoted to teaching writing in each subject area?

- Do teachers discuss writing as process with students?

- Are students asked to do extended writing assignments, or are they simply filling in the blanks?

- Do they have opportunities to revise?

- Are students exposed to distinct genres and types of writing tasks?

- How and when do teachers respond to student writing (grades, comments, conferences, and so forth)?

- Do teachers model writing or write with students?

- Are students encouraged to take risks in their writing?

- What inquiry strategies are being taught, and how are they embedded in writing assignments?

- Do students have opportunities to reflect on their progress and goals as writers?

- How are students evaluated in writing, and how well do they perform?

A Checklist for Administrators

To gauge the quality of writing instruction in the classroom, a school administrator can also use this checklist, updated from a 1982 American Association of School Administrators (AASA) Critical Issues Report, *Teaching Writing: Problems and Solutions.* Developed by Cecelia Kingston, a former language arts coordinator and district writing consultant in New York, to highlight "differences in instruction and outcome that occur when writing is simply *assigned* and when writing is authentically *taught,*" it has been adapted to reflect more current research on effective classroom practices.

When Writing Is Assigned	When Writing Is Taught
Teacher asks students to write on one topic from a list of topics that may or may not be related to course content or students' experiences.	Teacher encourages students to draw on prior knowledge and interests in their writing as a way to engage their thinking in authentic learning tasks.
Teacher selects writing topics for papers without consideration of their audience or purpose.	Audience and purpose for papers are specifically identified in assignments.
Students assume they are writing for a grade.	Students know they are writing for authentic communicative purposes.
Students are asked to write only on teacher-generated topics.	Students have opportunities to generate and develop topics that matter to them.
Students are given arbitrary time or word limits.	Students are asked to assess the scope or the purpose in terms of time available and word limits appropriate for writing task.
Students are required to hand in the first draft for a grade.	Students are encouraged to review and revise the first draft.
Teacher comments on paper are usually negative, most often correction of errors.	Teacher comments stress the positive and are constructive about the negative aspects.
Corrections are usually in reference to mechanical errors.	Suggestions for improvement in style, format, and organization of thought are made.
Usually the teacher corrects every error on every page.	Some errors are corrected for a specific assignment. Others are dealt with in conferences, minilessons, or peer-editing sessions.
Most of a teacher's time is spent correcting papers.	Most of a teacher's time is spent in class teaching writing skills and inquiry strategies.
Teachers correct every paper.	Teachers encourage self-evaluation and group evaluation of the papers.

When Writing Is Assigned	When Writing Is Taught
Students never quite know how a teacher arrives at a grade.	Students know why they earn a grade.
All writing assignments tend to be essays, usually 200–500 words, using a formulaic pattern such as the five-paragraph theme.	Students are taught how to handle distinct rhetorical elements appropriate to diverse writing genres whose length may vary according to the purpose of the assignment.
Students are asked to back up their opinions in their writing without regard for the quality or relevance of the support.	Students are taught strategies to assess the veracity of claims, the relevance of evidence, and the plausibility of inferences, and to apply these strategies to what they read and write.
Students are criticized for not making the purpose clear, for not organizing thoughts logically, for not developing ideas.	Assignments are designed with explicit steps to help students focus purpose, organize thoughts, and develop ideas with specific inquiry strategies.
Students are not aware of significant improvement in their writing.	Students reflect on significant growth, or lack of it, in specific writing skills.
Students are asked to analyze, compare, describe, narrate, review, and summarize, but they are not taught how to organize or elaborate ideas, or how to develop their characters, themes, or images.	Students are given writing models and assignments that guide them in how to develop their thinking and harness their imagination.
Students are required to rewrite—in some cases. But rewriting usually is limited to correcting grammar, usage, and so on.	Students are encouraged to revise, edit, and improve—and to correct drafts and then resubmit.
Students are required to write without much forethought.	Students are motivated to think about what they write through brainstorming, freewriting, role playing, discussion, or other prewriting activities.
Students rarely know what style means or what their own style is.	Students are encouraged to analyze and develop their own style and voice.
Students and teachers are bored by what students write.	Students and teachers are excited about what students write and make efforts to display and publish it.

Source: Adapted from S. B. Neil (ed.), *Teaching Writing: Problems and Solutions.* (AASA Critical Issues Report). Arlington, Va.: American Association of School Administrators, 1982. Used by permission.

P. David Pearson suggests that principals can best assess writing instruction by visiting classrooms, interviewing teachers, and looking at student work. Another means of collecting data about what's being emphasized in the classroom is to conduct a mini–research project with teachers, one that analyzes the learning objectives of a given week's lesson plan and then tracks how students actually spend their time on a particular day.

Build Flexibility, Community, and Long-Term Planning

It takes time to develop a schoolwide writing program. "The biggest mistake school districts make in implementing a writing program is not planning far enough ahead," according to Paul Eschholz, former director of the Vermont Writing Program. "It is a three- to five-year venture. Districts cannot expect to establish a program overnight and to have it functioning in two or three months. A writing program has to be introduced slowly and then built upon."[1]

In some school districts, the incubating period takes even longer to achieve results. Since the early 1980s, Maine has focused on writing as part of its effort to improve student literacy. The state has produced some of the nation's highest achievement in reading and writing and the highest percentage of students at or above the proficient level on NAEP assessments.[2] At a retreat in Bar Harbor, administrators from twelve high-achieving state school systems representing a variety of socioeconomic backgrounds were invited by the Maine Educational Assessment Committee to describe how they got the results they did. The length of time it took these schools to build their programs varied from five to eleven years.

Administrators in Maine credited the following factors for the success of their programs:

- Flexibility rather than orthodoxy in curriculum
- Respect for the teacher as a professional
- A sense of authentic school community
- Teamwork: participants with diverse experiences in the school system worked together to develop a common vision for improving literacy
- A bottom-up rather than top-down approach to developing the program

- Focus on learning results rather than test scores
- Low teacher turnover rate
- Investment in ongoing professional development

[In listening to administrators] I had expected to see more emphasis on specific instructional methodology as participant explanation for good student achievement. Instead, they emphasized general ways of organizing their work as very important. I was not sure whether the recurrent theme of flexibility was responsible for these answers, but it was evident that there was a sense that we needed to see literacy programs as much broader than specific materials or programs.

Connie Goldman, chair of the Maine Educational Assessment Committee, quoted in Donald H. Graves, *The Energy to Teach*, p. 112

Quite clearly, the growth in these [Maine school] systems was the near opposite of a top-down management system. At no point in these twelve systems were teachers bypassed or excluded from commitment.

Donald H. Graves, *The Energy to Teach*, p. 116

Make a Schoolwide Commitment

There is no single, absolutely correct leadership scenario for building a successful writing program. In some schools and districts, it begins with dialogue about writing guided by a curriculum coordinator, department chair, building principal, or language arts specialist. In others, a new curriculum is collectively spawned by a group of teachers. Linda Darling-Hammond and Donald H. Graves, among others, have studied how "blueprints for creating successful schools" and effective writing programs were devised and implemented.[3] Both argue that change cannot be achieved by top-down directives and that there are no overnight success stories. The rationale is clear: schoolwide improvement of writing requires collective buy-in—the willingness of teachers, administrators, and the community to comprehend and support the rationale for change. It evolves over time from shared commitment and understanding. Also required is a cadre of committed teachers with classroom experience in teaching writing who can share their knowledge of effective strategies. Finding experienced teachers who volunteer for the task, who write themselves, and who know the research in teaching writing is crucial to success.

Build Community Awareness

Exhibits are one way to broaden community awareness of writing; PTA and local school board presentations are another. A district or school should inform parents about changes in the writing program and expectations for student performance. Administrators can introduce new ideas about writing by having parents themselves write about school meetings and then involve them in the experience of drafting and revising. Another way to harness support is to develop a parents' guide for learning to write, or show a video of writing classrooms that highlight effective strategies. Administrators can provide leadership by showing that they value reading and writing themselves through their own writing. As Donald Graves suggests, if it is not valuable for us, why should it be for students? Parent writing workshops and book clubs are other ways to develop a larger dialogue about writing in the school community. Study groups, featuring guest speakers and teachers, can focus on issues such as phonics, the reading-and-writing connection, revision, peer response, techniques for reading aloud, writing genres, and inquiry strategies.

Administrators can provide leadership by showing
that they value reading and writing themselves
through their own writing.

Explore Effective Practices Through Ongoing Professional Development

In the successful writing program, the teacher has an opportunity to observe and discuss promising classroom practices. Current research in effective strategies is disseminated and used in workshop or discussion group settings. Sharing models of good writing assignments and student work, addressing issues such as paper load, graded and nongraded writing, and how to teach mechanics and formal aspects of writing in the context of authentic work and problem solving are part of the ongoing development of an effective writing program.

Administrators can offer available professional development resources to help faculty learn about effective practices and develop their knowledge and skills as writing teachers. For schools whose teachers have little experience teaching writing or writing themselves, professional development that focuses on getting participants to write and understand their own writing process often serves to energize teachers. They can then share what they have learned about writing with other faculty and staff. Ongoing in-service is essential; one two-hour session is insufficient.

As a recent survey of composition studies notes, "research and practice have shown that writing development is far from a linear process involving the acquisition of a set of discrete skills."[4] Teaching writing should be informed by developmental awareness. It starts by engaging young writers in rich, natural-language experiences and proceeds to more complex kinds of thinking and problem solving. An effective writing program evolves a coherent, localized sense of the students' developing needs as writers. This is the antithesis of a rigid, scope-and-sequence, one-size-fits-all model. Rather, it is based on careful observation of individual student needs and passed on through grade levels. As a school builds its program, teachers from diverse disciplines are involved in constructing the writing curriculum. Consistent standards and expectations are developed through ongoing discussion and sharing of information about student needs so that they can gain proficiency with ever more challenging writing tasks.

As a school builds its program,
teachers from diverse disciplines are involved
in constructing the writing curriculum.
Consistent standards and expectations are
developed through ongoing discussion and sharing
of information about student needs.

Promote Writing Across the Curriculum

As a movement, writing across the curriculum was inspired by the research of James Britton and Nancy Martin and others at the University of London's Schools Council Project[5] and by efforts to integrate it in England's schools beginning in the 1960s. It is a burgeoning movement in the United States, and the scope and purpose of such curricula vary greatly in secondary to postsecondary schools. To some, they exemplify the most innovative instructional models on the educational horizon,[6] but even proponents acknowledge that institutional resistance can be enormous, and rigorous assessment has not generally been a priority.[7]

Although many elementary school teachers use writing across the curriculum to enhance learning in diverse subjects, it is less commonly applied in secondary education, where learning is so heavily focused on content. Two exceptions are International High School in Manhattan and Hudson High School, described in the case studies later in this chapter. They share a common assumption that writing is a part of all content areas rather than a discrete subject. Administrators can support this approach by offering in-service training and creating opportunities for teachers and staff to observe such programs in action. Administrators can also encourage teachers in diverse subject areas to discuss how to use writing as a tool for inquiry, critical thinking, and active learning.

Previous chapters have explored how elementary and middle schools can use writing to learn and create an effective writing program. The following case studies show how writing can also enhance learning at the secondary level, where, in P. David Pearson's phrase, "content is king."

CASE STUDY
Building a Schoolwide Writing Program at Hudson High—A Superintendent's Story

Hudson High School in Massachusetts is one of the more remarkable success stories in the annals of current education reform. In the mid-1990s, Hudson's district superintendent, Sheldon Berman, began thinking about how writing could be used to advance his whole-school reform efforts. It would lead him to implement a schoolwide, writing-across-the-curriculum program. Today, Berman says he believes in "doing what is right for kids," even if it diverges from some of the state's standards. "We looked carefully at the state's expectations, and frankly, we preferred earlier versions of

You get some pretty dramatic results when you get teachers in conversations about student work that are deep and built around common expectations and standards. Teachers are learning to speak the language of writing, which is to talk to kids about what revising looks like, to talk about what kids mean and want to say, to help them understand what peer editing looks like—not just in correcting spelling and punctuation.

Maddie Brick,
ELA coordinator, Hudson Schools

its curriculum frameworks. What we've done is take the best out of the standards, and my role as district superintendent has been to protect people from some of the negative changes."

Berman saw writing as an engine for the districtwide goals he'd worked hard to get his local school committee to approve: "progressive, student-active, inquiry-oriented teaching." But he faced formidable obstacles, familiar to many school administrators. Hudson High School (HHS), whose year 2000 enrollment stood at 916 students with eighty-eight full-time faculty, had experienced extensive, retirement-driven attrition, resulting in a 60 percent teaching staff turnover since 1996. To recruit new teachers, Berman placed this job posting for the type of teacher he and his administrative staff believed would thrive in their reform environment:

> The Hudson Public School system is looking for creative, student-centered, and technologically literate teachers committed to working in a culturally and economically diverse community. We are interested in educators who engage students in cooperative learning, service learning, critical thinking, problem solving, and character education, and who are interested in innovative instructional approaches.

Berman hired a group of dynamic curriculum directors committed to creating a faculty culture where improving writing would be a priority for all teachers. A key goal was to build links between curricular areas.

Berman's leadership and the steps taken by his associates in the school and community "transformed Hudson High from a very traditional, quietly underperforming school into a model of education reform."[8] Maddie Brick, Berman's English language arts coordinator for grades 6–12, began the process by surveying Hudson teachers to find out which student needs they felt were the highest priorities. Writing, they all agreed, was the most challenging task for both students and teachers. Brick brought together a cadre of teachers interested in tackling the problem and got a grant to send them to a writing institute, then later to work with Peter Elbow, director of the writing program at the University of Massachusetts, Amherst. Elbow asked these Hudson teachers to look at their own writing, and to share and discuss their own process as writers. It would help them to better understand what kids need to know and do to develop as writers.

This core of committed teachers and ongoing professional development in teaching writing laid the groundwork for a schoolwide writing-across-the-curriculum program at HHS. The same core group became teacher leaders, initiating faculty discussion about expectations and standards for good writing across content areas. A strong emphasis was placed on expository, persuasive, and analytical writing. Teachers at Hudson began writing with their students in class and bringing in their own work for discussion as a way of modeling the process. Samples of student work in a variety of genres were collected for the specific purpose of creating a rubric and establishing consistent expectations that everyone in the school community could recognize as a common standard.

In 2001, Hudson High School was one of ten Massachusetts schools to receive a Vanguard Award from the Mass Insight Education and Research Institute (MIERI), a nonprofit public policy group of business leaders and school superintendents who advocate for higher standards and education reform. The award was based in part on three years of steady improvement in language arts and math as measured by student performance on the Massachusetts Comprehensive Assessment System and California Achievement Tests. HHS was the only high school in the state to receive the award.

The ability to articulate ideas is something all of our curriculum directors focused on. It's become a key to science, a key to math. We looked for opportunities for students to relay their thinking and delineate it, whether it's in a journal, in explaining their answers, or in the write-up of an experiment or investigation. We're continually asking students to do more writing because of its critical nature.

Sheldon Berman,
district superintendent, Hudson Schools

Hudson High School's Writing Program

To build an effective schoolwide writing program, Hudson High School's staff and teachers did the following:

- Focused on improving writing as an overall school reform goal

- Engaged in an ongoing dialogue about writing as both a tool for learning and an overarching element of the curriculum

- Attended workshops on writing and the teaching of writing

- Analyzed their own writing experiences to better understand students' development and needs as writers

- Collected and shared effective teaching practices

- Created and compared their own syllabi for course work

- Provided student-centered writing instruction

- Wrote and revised with students in class

- Assigned daily writing in some subjects

- Established consistent expectations and common standards for writing

- Created assessment rubrics with students that covered distinct writing genres

CASE STUDY
Writing at International High School

Teachers at Manhattan's innovative International High School created a schoolwide writing-across-the-curriculum program to meet the needs of a highly diverse student body. Their common bond was that English was not their native language. But their teachers understood that gaining proficiency in writing was crucial to their success both in academia and in the professional world. More and more students whose home language is not English are entering classrooms, including those at the postsecondary and graduate levels, where full English proficiency is expected or presumed. They may have achieved varying degrees of oral proficiency, but inattention to their writing skills will leave them underprepared. Teachers often do not understand their specific instructional needs, or they may assume that writing can only be taught to students who are English language learners *after* they have achieved oral proficiency. At International High School, teachers were determined to show how students with limited English language proficiency could achieve high performance in all content areas. In 1996–97, the school was part of a national study that focused on English instruction at twenty-five innovative and exemplary middle and high schools.[9] This case study is adapted from a recent CELA report authored by Paola Bonissone for Judith Langer's Excellence in English research project.[10]

International High School (IHS) was established in 1985 by the New York State Board of Education for students who were recent immigrants. These students had been in the United States less than four years and scored below the 21st percentile on the Language Assessment Battery. Currently 450 students are enrolled at IHS. In 1997–98 they represented forty-eight countries and spoke thirty-seven languages. Eighty percent were eligible for free or reduced lunch.

The school uses innovative writing-across-the-curriculum programs and a complex portfolio assessment system that encourages students to reflect on their own development as writers. The assessment must also show that each student has met or exceeded all content and skill requirements outlined in state standards. As Judith Langer notes, IHS students "are actively involved in becoming highly literate; they are learning how language works in context and how to use it to advantage for academic purposes."[11]

According to Linda Darling-Hammond, "in a traditional New York City high school, most of these students would drop out before 12th grade."[12] But International has a remarkable track record: for ten years it has graduated "virtually all of its students, enabling them to pass both the New York State competency tests and a set of much more rigorous performance assessments developed within the school."[13] In the 1995–96 school year, 91.8 percent of its graduates were accepted by Columbia, Cornell, MIT, and various state universities and community colleges. Since many of the students arrive speaking little or no English, mentoring and coaching help students achieve proficiency. All new students are paired with a student of the same first language so they can help each other by using their native language. Students work collaboratively:

> Teenagers who are recent immigrants to the United States can be seen clustered around lab tables, talking and gesturing intently as they work out a physics problem. . . . [They] communicate successfully with one another using sketches, mathematical notations, role playing, and phrases in English and their native languages. . . . In another classroom, pairs of students are reading each other's biographies and asking questions to guide revisions. Before they are done, they will have revised their writing several times to refine their ideas and clarity of expression. A student from Ghana asks one from Puerto Rico if she can explain more about the culture of San Juan in her autobiography. As these two converse, they are learning about other societies, expanding their view of the world, building a new relationship, and developing their ability to communicate.[14]

The school offers a thematically arranged interdisciplinary curriculum. Approximately seventy students are assigned to one of six thematic programs. Each program has two themes, one for each semester, taught by a team of five to seven humanities and science, math, or technology teachers. The curriculum is planned and developed by the faculty, and students work in collaborative groups, using teacher-written activity guides rather than textbooks as they explore study topics from one of these programs:

• "American Dream" and "American Reality"
• "Motion" and "Visibility/Invisibility"
• "Crime and Punishment" and "City Life"

- "It's Your World" and "Conflict and Resolution"
- "World of Money" and "World Around Us"
- "Origins and Structures"

Writing is embedded in the IHS culture for both teachers and students. It is a part of all student projects, including those in science, math, and technology. In the Origins and Structures program, writing is the principal way ideas are shared, expanded, and learned. Drawing from activity guides created by instructors, students write in various formats and genres, from a short paragraph explaining what they have done to a longer essay expressing what they have learned. This work supports the schoolwide goal of building such language skills as vocabulary development, grammar, and writing in various genres. Teachers use writing to generate their own guidelines, procedures, grant proposals, and self-assessment. Teachers participate in "peer evaluation team" reviews in which they present portfolios of their work as a means to assess their own performance.

Emphasis is placed on making connections between themes and content across disciplines. For example, students in the Origins and Structures program wrote about mythology for their humanities class as they constructed three-dimensional temples using mathematical concepts learned in science class. International High School successfully integrates writing in all aspects of learning, including assessment. Teaching and learning to write are based on these strategies:

> At International, writing is viewed as a way to construct understanding and develop language. Writing is considered important and students are encouraged to use it to explain their thoughts and what they have learned. . . . In other places, non-native students often do less writing than their native peers because their oral language skills may not be as proficient as what is perceived to be necessary in order to write. This is not the case in International's writing culture, where everyone is viewed as a writer, and no one is deprived of this essential learning tool.
>
> Paola Bonissone, *Teaming to Teach English to International High School Students: A Case Study,* p. 26

Writing across the curriculum. A teacher in the Origins and Structures program notes, "One of the reasons that we're having kids do so much writing is that there is a schoolwide concern that we really use writing in the mathematics and science classroom. The other is that [through the writing] we can see what ideas the students really comprehend and where they are faltering."

Direct and indirect learning. In the Origins and Structures program, writing assignments are designed to focus on science content, but through them students gain vocabulary, learn mechanics, and gain experience with various writing tasks. They all reflect on their learning and make connections among disciplines.

Extensive oral and written feedback. Comments are a key part of how the teacher interacts with students, and they are often given on work in progress. Generally they take the form of questions about specific content, or directions to students to reflect on or reconsider points they have just made. Less often, they address specific points of grammar or organization. With comments on how to improve work, grades are assigned, but students may always return to and revise their writing.

Student ownership of learning through writing. As Alison McCluer, who has taught at International for nine years, observes, "Students take more responsibility for their learning when they need to write about it. It may be that it helps them realize what it is that they're not really clear about. It certainly helps you the teacher to see what they're having difficulty with."

These two case studies illustrate how schools can successfully meet the challenge of improving student writing as described in the opening chapter of this book. They demonstrate how writing can be a powerful means for achieving high standards and expectations for learning by all students. These schools did so by making a schoolwide commitment to writing as a focus for improving instruction and student achievement in all subject areas. What Richard Elmore calls "a culture of shared values," with a focus on high-quality instruction, lies at the core of their success. But as he cautions, simple exhortations to improve instruction are not enough. Administrators can foster a climate for change and new ideas by drawing on the primary resource for deep and sustained educational reform: teacher expertise and support for best practices.

Meeting the writing challenge requires a paradigm shift away from the limited view of writing as a discrete subject area or the exclusive domain of English language arts instruction. Because writing can support a high level of learning in all core subjects, it matters in any classroom where inquiry, knowledge, and expression are valued and recognized by students and teachers. Schools that harness writing as an essential tool for learning know the benefits of giving students the skills and confidence to be better writers. Writing helps students become better readers and thinkers. It can help students reflect critically about the information and ideas they must understand and make use of both in academia and in the world outside its doors. It can improve achievement in school and in the professions students aspire to. It supports their growth as adult independent thinkers. Writing is a gateway to students' emerging role in our nation's future as participants and decision makers in a democratic society. This is why writing matters and why improving it should be a goal in all our schools.

NOTES

Introduction

1. Rose, M. *Possible Lives.* New York: Penguin, 1985.
2. Connors, R. J. *Composition-Rhetoric: Backgrounds, Theory, and Pedagogy.* (Pittsburgh Series in Composition, Literacy, and Culture). Pittsburgh, Pa.: University of Pittsburgh Press, 1997.
3. Applebee, A. N. "Alternative Models of Writing Development." In R. Indrisano and J. R. Squire (eds.), *Perspectives on Writing: Research, Theory, and Practice.* Newark, Del.: International Reading Association, 2000, p. 90.
4. Strickland, D. S., Bodino, A., Buchan, K., Jones, K. M., Nelson, A., and Rosen, M. "Teaching Writing in a Time of Reform." *Elementary School Journal,* 2001, *101*(4), 388.
5. Sheils, M. "Why Johnny Can't Write." *Newsweek,* Dec. 8, 1975, pp. 58–63.
6. *Becoming a Nation of Readers: The Report of the Commission on Reading.* Washington, D.C.: National Institute of Education, U.S. Department of Education, 1985.
7. Lewin, T. "College Board Announces an Overhaul for the SAT." *New York Times,* June 28, 2002, p. A12.
8. Cavanagh, S. "Overhauled SAT Could Shake Up School Curricula." *Education Week,* July 10, 2002, p. 28.

Chapter One

1. Winokur, J. (ed.) *Advice to Writers.* New York: Vintage Books, 1999, p. 107.
2. Graves, R. L. (ed.). *Writing, Teaching, Learning: A Sourcebook.* Portsmouth, N.H.: Boynton/Cook, 1999.
3. White, S. *The NAEP 1998 Reading Report Card: National and State Highlights.* (NCES 1999–479). Washington, D.C.: National Center for Education Statistics,

Office of Educational Research and Improvement, U.S. Department of Education, 1999, p. 10.

4. Author interview with Donald Murray, July 30, 2001.

5. Freedman, S. W., Flower, L., Hull, G., and Hayes, J. R. "Ten Years of Research: Achievements of the National Center for the Study of Writing and Literacy." (Technical report no. 1-C). Berkeley, Calif.: National Center for the Study of Writing, 1995.

6. Author interview with Crystal England, Aug. 14, 2001.

7. Hillocks, G., Jr. *The Testing Trap.* New York: Teachers College Press, 2002.

8. Wiggins, G. *Educative Assessment.* San Francisco: Jossey-Bass, 1998.

9. Applebee, A. N. "Alternative Models of Writing Development." In R. Indrisano and J. R. Squire (eds.), *Perspectives on Writing: Research, Theory, and Practice.* Newark, Del.: International Reading Association, 2000, p. 92.

10. See discussion of strategies in Hillocks, G., Jr. *Teaching Writing as Reflective Practice.* New York: Teachers College Press, 1995, pp. 99–110 and 219–223.

11. Elbow, P. *Everyone Can Write: Essays Toward a Hopeful Theory of Writing and Teaching Writing.* New York: Oxford University Press, 2000, pp. xiv–xv.

Chapter Two

1. James Berlin, quoted in M. Rose, *Possible Lives.* New York: Penguin, 1985, p. 208.

2. Rose, 1985.

3. Quoted in M. Rose, "The Language of Exclusion." In V. Villanueva, Jr. (ed.), *Cross-Talk in Composition Theory: A Reader.* Urbana, Ill.: National Council of Teachers of English, 1997, p. 529.

4. King, J. A. "Seeing Common Ground: A Parent's Guide to Process Writing Instruction and Assessment." Unpublished manuscript, 1997. Used by permission of Julie A. King.

5. *Becoming a Nation of Readers: The Report of the Commission on Reading.* Washington, D.C.: National Institute of Education, U.S. Department of Education, 1985.

6. Elley, W. B., Barham, I. H., Lamb, H., and Wyllie, M. *The Role of Grammar in a Secondary School Curriculum.* Wellington: New Zealand Council of Educational Research, 1979; Hillocks, G., Jr. *Research on Written Composition.* Urbana, Ill.: National Conference on Research in English, 1986; Freedman, S. W., and Daiute, C. "Instructional Methods and Learning in Teaching Writing." In *Subject-Specific Instructional Activities and Methods.* Vol. 8. New York: Elsevier Science, 2001.

7. Emig, J. *The Web of Meaning: Essays on Writing, Teaching, Learning, and Thinking.* Portsmouth, N.H.: Boynton/Cook, 1983.

8. Hillocks, G., Jr. *The Testing Trap.* New York: Teachers College Press, 2002, p. 200.

9. Hillocks, G., Jr. *Teaching Writing as Reflective Practice.* New York: Teachers College Press, 1995.

10. Bean, J. C. *Engaging Ideas: The Professor's Guide to Integrating Writing, Critical Thinking, and Active Learning in the Classroom.* San Francisco: Jossey-Bass, 1996, pp. 131–132. Used by permission of John Wiley & Sons, Inc.

11. Sperling, M., and Freedman, S. W. "Teaching Writing." In V. Richardson (ed.), *Handbook of Research on Teaching.* New York: Macmillan, 2001. (Sponsored by American Educational Research Association).

12. Flower, L. S., and Hayes, J. R. "A Cognitive Process Theory of Writing." *College Composition and Communication,* 1981, *32*(4), 365–387; Hayes, J. R., and Flower, L. S. "Identifying the Organization of Writing Processes." In L. W. Gregg and E. R. Steinberg (eds.), *Cognitive Process in Writing.* Hillsdale, N.J.: Erlbaum, 1980.

13. Tracy Kidder, conversation with the author, 1995.

14. Heath, S. B. *Ways with Words: Language, Life, and Work in Communities and Classrooms.* New York: Cambridge University Press, 1983.

15. Taylor, D., and Dorsey-Gaines, C. *Growing Up Literate: Learning from Inner-City Families.* Portsmouth, N.H.: Heinemann, 1988.

16. Freeman, D. E., and Freeman, Y. S. *Between Worlds: Access to Second Language Acquisition.* Portsmouth, N.H.: Heinemann, 1994, p. 3.

17. National Research Council. *Preventing Reading Difficulties in Young Children.* (C. E. Snow, M. S. Burns, and P. Griffin, eds.). Washington, D.C.: National Academy Press, 1998.

18. Dyson, A. H. *Multiple Worlds of Child Writers: Friends Learning to Write.* New York: Teachers College Press, 1989; Dyson, A. H. *Social Worlds of Children Learning to Write in an Urban Primary School.* New York: Teachers College Press, 1992.

19. Dyson, 1992, p. 4.

20. Freedman, S. W., and Daiute, C. "Instructional Methods and Learning in Teaching Writing." In *Subject-Specific Instructional Activities and Methods.* Vol. 8. New York: Elsevier Science, 2001.

21. Dyson, A. H., and Freedman, S. W. "On Teaching Writing: A Review of the Literature." (Occasional paper no. 20). Berkeley, Calif.: National Center for the Study of Writing, 1990.

22. Freedman, S. W., Flower, L., Hull, G., and Hayes, J. R. "Ten Years of Research: Achievements of the National Center for the Study of Writing and Literacy." (Technical report no. 1-C). Berkeley, Calif.: National Center for the Study of Writing, 1995, p. 9.

23. Langer, J., and Flihan, S. "Writing and Reading Relationships: Constructive

Tasks." In R. Indrisano and J. R. Squire (eds.), *Perspectives on Writing: Research, Theory, and Practice.* Newark, Del.: International Reading Association, 2000, p. 127.

24. Stotsky, S. "Research on Reading/Writing Relationships: A Synthesis and Suggested Directions." *Language Arts,* 1983, *60*(5), 636.

25. Tompkins is quoted in National Writing Project, *Profiles of the National Writing Project: Improving Writing in the Nation's Schools.* Berkeley, Calif.: National Writing Project, 1999.

26. Gavelek, J. P., Raphael, T. E., Biondo, S. M., and Wang, D. "Integrated Literacy Instruction." In M. L. Kamil, P. B. Mosenthal, D. B. Pearson, and R. Barr (eds.), *Handbook of Reading Research.* Vol. 3. Mahwah, N.J.: Erlbaum, 2000; Pearson, D. P. "Integrated Language Arts: Sources of Controversy and Seeds of Consensus." In L. M. Morrow, J. K. Smith, and L. C. Wilkinson (eds.), *Integrated Language Arts: Controversy to Consensus.* Boston: Allyn & Bacon, 1994.

27. Sheils, M. "Why Johnny Can't Write." *Newsweek,* Dec. 8, 1975, pp. 58–63.

28. Burke, J. *The English Teacher's Companion: A Complete Guide to Classroom, Curriculum, and the Profession.* Portsmouth, N.H.: Boynton/Cook, 1999.

29. Delpit, L. *Other People's Children: Cultural Conflict in the Classroom.* New York: New Press, 1995.

30. Delpit, 1995, p. 19.

31. Delpit, 1995, p. 62.

32. Applebee, A. N. *Writing in the Secondary School: English and the Content Areas.* (Research monograph 21). Urbana, Ill.: National Council of Teachers of English, 1981; Applebee, A. N. *Contexts for Learning to Write: Studies of Secondary School Instruction.* Norwood, N.J.: Ablex, 1984.

33. Applebee, A. N. "Alternative Models of Writing Development." In R. Indrisano and J. R. Squire (eds.), *Perspectives on Writing: Research, Theory, and Practice.* Newark, Del.: International Reading Association, 2000, p. 91.

34. Applebee, 2000, p. 92.

35. Langer, J. *Beating the Odds: Teaching Middle and High School Students to Read and Write Well.* (CELA report no. 12014). Albany, N.Y.: National Center on English Learning and Achievement, 1999; Langer, J. *Guidelines for Teaching Middle and High School Students to Read and Write Well: Six Features of Effective Instruction.* Albany, N.Y.: National Center on English Learning and Achievement, 2000; Manning, T. *Achieving High-Quality Reading and Writing in an Urban Middle School: The Case of Gail Slatko.* (CELA report no. 13001). Albany, N.Y.: National Center on English Learning and Achievement, 2000.

36. Manning, 2000, p. 5.

37. Manning, 2000, p. 2.

38. Langer, 2000, p. 5.
39. Langer, 2000, p. 5.

Chapter Three

1. Greenwald, E. A., Persky, H. R., Campbell, J. R., and Mazzeo, J. *NAEP 1998 Writing Report Card for the Nation and the States.* (NCES 1999–462). Washington, D.C.: National Center for Education Statistics, Office of Educational Research and Improvement, U.S. Department of Education, 1999.

2. National Center for Education Statistics. "Can Students Benefit from Process Writing?" (NCES 96–845). *NAEPfacts,* 1996, *1*(3).

3. Hillocks, G., Jr. *Research on Written Composition.* Urbana, Ill.: National Conference on Research in English, 1986, p. 28.

4. Applebee, A. N., Langer, J. A., and Mullis, I.V.S. *The Writing Report Card: Writing Achievement in America's Schools.* (ETS Report no. 15-W-02). Princeton, N.J.: Educational Testing Service and National Assessment of Educational Progress, 1986; Greenwald, Persky, Campbell, and Mazzeo, 1999.

5. Storms, B., Gentile, C., Riazantseva, A., and Eidman-Aadahl, E. *Analyzing Classroom Writing Assignments: Lessons Learned from the 1998 Classroom Writing Study.* Princeton, N.J.: Educational Testing Service and National Writing Project, 2000.

6. Academy for Educational Development. *National Writing Project Evaluation: NWP Classrooms: Strategies, Assignments and Student Work. Year Two Results.* New York: Academy for Educational Development, 2002.

7. Newmann, F. M., Byrk, A. S., and Nagaoka, J. K. *Authentic Intellectual Work and Standardized Tests: Conflict or Coexistence?* Chicago: Consortium on Chicago School Research, 2001, p. 14.

8. Newmann, Byrk, and Nagaoka, 2001, p. 25.

9. Academy for Educational Development. *National Writing Project Evaluation: NWP Classrooms: Strategies, Assignments and Student Work. Year One Results.* New York: Academy for Educational Development, 2001, pp. 31, 36.

10. Tierney, R. "Using Expressive Writing to Teach Biology." (Appendix D). In A. Wotring and R. Tierney (eds.), *Two Studies of Writing in High School Science.* Berkeley: Bay Area Writing Project, University of California, 1981, pp. 149–150.

11. Tierney, 1981, p. 163.

12. Hillocks, G., Jr. *Teaching Writing as Reflective Practice.* New York: Teachers College Press, 1995, p. 100.

13. Hillocks, 1995, pp. 105–106.

14. Hillocks, G., Jr. *The Testing Trap.* New York: Teachers College Press, 2002, p. 172.

Chapter Four

1. Daniels, H., Bizar, M., and Zemelman, S. *Rethinking High School: Best Practice in Teaching, Learning, and Leadership.* Portsmouth, N.H.: Heinemann, 2001.

2. McLaughlin, M. W., and Talbert, J. E. "Contexts That Matter for Teaching and Learning: Strategic Opportunities for Meeting the Nation's Education Goals." (Research report). Stanford, Calif.: Center for Research on the Context of Secondary School Teaching, 1993.

3. Elmore, R. F. "Building a New Structure for School Leadership." Paper for Albert Shanker Institute, Washington, D.C., 2000, p. 28.

4. Fullan, M. *Leading in a Culture of Change.* San Francisco: Jossey-Bass, 2001.

5. Adapted from R. F. Elmore, *Investing in Teacher Learning: Staff Development and Instructional Improvement in Community School District #2, New York City.* New York: National Commission on Teaching and America's Future, Aug. 1997, pp. 8–13. Reprinted with permission of the National Commission on Teaching and America's Future.

6. National Association of Elementary School Principals. *Leading Learning Communities: NAESP Standards for What Principals Should Know and Be Able to Do.* Alexandria, Va.: National Association of Elementary School Principals, 2001.

7. Daniels, Bizar, and Zemelman, 2001.

8. Darling-Hammond, L. *The Right to Learn: A Blueprint for Creating Schools That Work.* San Francisco: Jossey-Bass, 1997, p. 184, Table 6.2, and p. 209, n. 1.

9. Elmore, 1997, pp. 13–30.

10. Harwayne, S. *Writing Through Childhood: Rethinking Process and Product.* Portsmouth, N.H.: Heinemann, 2001, pp. 239–240.

11. Gray, J. *Teachers at the Center: A Memoir of the Early Years of the National Writing Project.* Berkeley, Calif.: National Writing Project, 2000, p. 103.

12. Lieberman, A., and Wood, D. R. "The National Writing Project." *Educational Leadership,* 2002, *59*(6), 40.

13. Gray, 2000, p. 85.

14. National Writing Project. *Profiles of the National Writing Project: Improving Writing in the Nation's Schools.* Berkeley, Calif.: National Writing Project, 1999.

15. Gray, 2000, p. 103.

16. Check, J. "Imaginary Gardens and Real Issues: Improving Language Arts in the Urban Elementary School." *Quarterly of the National Writing Project,* 2000, *22*(1), 2–7, 31–38. Available on-line: [http://nwp.edgateway.net/cs/nwpp/view/nwpr140]. Used by permission of the National Writing Project.

Chapter Five

1. Strickland, D. S., Bodino, A., Buchan, K., Jones, K. M., Nelson, A., and Rosen, M. "Teaching Writing in a Time of Reform." *Elementary School Journal,* 2001, *101*(4), 388.

2. Strickland and others, 2001, p. 390.

3. "Standard Four." In International Reading Association and National Council of Teachers of English, *Standards for the Assessment of Reading and Writing.* Urbana, Ill.: National Council of Teachers of English, 1994.

4. Millman, R. S. "Using Writing to Assess Mathematics Pedagogy and Students' Understanding." In C. R. Cooper and L. Odell (eds.), *Evaluating Writing: The Role of Teachers' Knowledge About Text, Learning, and Culture.* Urbana, Ill.: National Council of Teachers of English, 1999.

5. Millman, 1999, p. 166.

6. Hillocks, G., Jr. *Teaching Writing as Reflective Practice.* New York: Teachers College Press, 1995, p. 107.

7. Mencken, K. "When All Meets All." *NABE News,* May–June 2001, pp. 4–7.

8. Mencken, 2001, p. 5.

9. Hoff, D. J. "Teaching, Standards, Tests Found Not Aligned." *Education Week,* Oct. 31, 2001, *21*(9). [www.edweek.org/ew/browse_ew_21.htm].

10. Hillocks, G., Jr. *The Testing Trap.* New York: Teachers College Press, 2002, p. 6.

11. Hillocks, 2002.

12. Hillocks, 2002, p. 64.

13. Hillocks, 2002, pp. 114, 136.

14. Elley, W. B., Barham, I. H., Lamb, H., and Wyllie, M. *The Role of Grammar in a Secondary School Curriculum.* Wellington: New Zealand Council of Educational Research, 1979; Hillocks, G., Jr. *Research on Written Composition.* Urbana, Ill.: National Conference on Research in English, 1986; Freedman, S. W., and Daiute, C. "Instructional Methods and Learning in Teaching Writing." In *Subject-Specific Instructional Activities and Methods.* Vol. 8. New York: Elsevier Science, 2001.

15. Freedman and Daiute, 2001, p. 106.

16. Murphy, S., and Smith, M. A. "Creating a Climate for Portfolios." In C. R. Cooper and L. Odell (eds.), *Evaluating Writing: The Role of Teachers' Knowledge About Text, Learning, and Culture.* Urbana, Ill.: National Council of Teachers of English, 1999.

17. Wiggins, G. *Educative Assessment.* San Francisco: Jossey-Bass, 1998, p. 163.

18. Wiggins, 1998, p. 163.

19. Hillocks, 2002, p. 112.

20. Bereiter, C., and Scardamalia, M. *The Psychology of Written Composition.* Hillsdale, N.J.: Erlbaum, 1987; Camp, R. "Portfolio Reflections in Middle and

Secondary School Classrooms." In K. B. Yancey (ed.), *Portfolios in the Writing Classroom: An Introduction.* Urbana, Ill.: National Council of Teachers of English, 1992, pp. 61–79.

21. New Standards Project. *Student Portfolio Handbook: Middle School English Arts Field Trial Version.* Washington, D.C.: National Center on Education and the Economy, and Pittsburgh, Pa.: Learning, Research, and Development Center, University of Pittsburgh, 1994.

22. Hillocks, 2002, p. 194.

23. Hillocks, 2002, p. 54.

24. Hillocks, 2002, p. 205.

25. Hillocks, 2002, p. 197.

26. Meyer, L., Orlofsky, G. F., Skinner, R. A., and Spicer, S. "The State of the States." In *Quality Counts 2002.* (Special report). *Education Week,* Jan. 10, 2002, *21*(17), 68–94. Available on-line: [www.edweek.org/sreports/qc02/].

Chapter Six

1. Quoted in Neil, S. B. (ed.). *Teaching Writing: Problems and Solutions.* (AASA Critical Issues report). Arlington, Va.: American Association of School Administrators, 1982.

2. Greenwald, E. A., Persky, H. R., Campbell, J. R., and Mazzeo, J. *NAEP 1998 Writing Report Card for the Nation and the States.* (NCES 1999–462). Washington, D.C.: National Center for Education Statistics, Office of Educational Research and Improvement, U.S. Department of Education, 1999, pp. 112–114, Figures 5.2 and 5.3.

3. Darling-Hammond, L. *The Right to Learn: A Blueprint for Creating Schools That Work.* San Francisco: Jossey-Bass, 1997; Graves, D. H. *The Energy to Teach.* Portsmouth, N.H.: Heinemann, 2001.

4. Freedman, S. W., and Daiute, C. "Instructional Methods and Learning in Teaching Writing." In *Subject-Specific Instructional Activities and Methods.* Vol. 8. New York: Elsevier Science, 2001.

5. Britton, J., Burgess, T., Martin, N., McLeod, A., and Rosen, H. *The Development of Writing Abilities (11–18).* London: Macmillan, 1975.

6. Coles, W. E., Jr. "Writing Across the Curriculum: Why Bother?" *Rhetoric Society Quarterly,* 1991, *21,* 17–25; Bonissone, P. R. *Teaming to Teach English to International High School Students: A Case Study.* (CELA report no. 13005). Albany, N.Y.: National Center on English Learning and Achievement, 2000.

7. Olds, B. M., Leydens, J. A., and Miller, R. L. "A Flexible Model for Assessing WAC Programs." *Journal of Language and Learning Across the Disciplines,* 1999, *3*(2), 123–129. [http://aw.colostate.edu/llad/issues.htm]; Young, A. "The Wonder of Writing Across the Curriculum." *Journal of Language and Learning Across the Disciplines,* 1994, *1*(1), 58–71. [http://aw.colostate.edu/llad/issues.htm].

8. Calkins, A. J. *Uncommon Wisdom: Effective Reform Strategies from the 2001 Vanguard Schools.* (Summary profiles). Boston: Mass Insight Education, 2001.

9. Langer, J. *Beating the Odds: Teaching Middle and High School Students to Read and Write Well.* (CELA report no. 12014). Albany, N.Y.: National Center on English Learning and Achievement, 1999.

10. Bonissone, 2000.

11. Judith Langer, in Bonissone, 2000, p. 1.

12. Darling-Hammond, L. *The Right to Learn: A Blueprint for Creating Schools That Work.* San Francisco: Jossey-Bass, 1997, p. 3.

13. Darling-Hammond, 1997, p. 3.

14. Darling-Hammond, 1997, p. 2.

BIBLIOGRAPHY

In addition to the works cited below, the following educators and researchers are quoted in the text from interviews or personal communications with the author: Sheldon Berman, Maddie Brick, Joe Check, Donald Graves, Donald Murray, Kate Nolan, P. David Pearson, Bob Petersen, Sherry Swain, B. J. Wagner, and Steve Zemelman.

Academy for Educational Development. *National Writing Project Evaluation. NWP Classrooms: Strategies, Assignments and Student Work. Year One Results.* New York: Academy for Educational Development, 2001.

Academy for Educational Development. *National Writing Project Evaluation. NWP Classrooms: Strategies, Assignments and Student Work. Year Two Results.* New York: Academy for Educational Development, 2002.

Applebee, A. N. *Writing in the Secondary School: English and the Content Areas.* (Research monograph no. 21). Urbana, Ill.: National Council of Teachers of English, 1981.

Applebee, A. N. *Contexts for Learning to Write: Studies of Secondary School Instruction.* Norwood, N.J.: Ablex, 1984.

Applebee, A. N. "Alternative Models of Writing Development." In R. Indrisano and J. R. Squire (eds.), *Perspectives on Writing: Research, Theory, and Practice.* Newark, Del.: International Reading Association, 2000.

Applebee, A. N., Langer, J. A., and Mullis, I.V.S. *The Writing Report Card: Writing Achievement in America's Schools.* (ETS Report no. 15-W-02). Princeton, N.J.: Educational Testing Service and National Assessment of Educational Progress, 1986.

Applebee, A. N., Langer, J. A., Mullis, I.V.S., Latham, A. S., and Gentile, C. A. *NAEP 1992 Writing Report Card.* Washington, D.C.: National Center for Education Statistics, Office of Educational Research and Improvement, U.S. Department of Education, 1994.

Bean, J. C. *Engaging Ideas: The Professor's Guide to Integrating Writing, Critical Thinking, and Active Learning in the Classroom.* San Francisco: Jossey-Bass, 1996.

Becoming a Nation of Readers: The Report of the Commission on Reading. Washington, D.C.: National Institute of Education, U.S. Department of Education, 1985.

Bereiter, C., and Scardamalia, M. *The Psychology of Written Composition.* Hillsdale, N.J.: Erlbaum, 1987.

Blau, S. "The Only Thing New Under the Sun: Twenty-Five Years of the National Writing Project." *Quarterly of the National Writing Project,* 1999, *21*(3), 2–7, 32.

Bonissone, P. R. *Teaming to Teach English to International High School Students: A Case Study.* (CELA report no. 13005). Albany, N.Y.: National Center on English Learning and Achievement, 2000.

Britton, J., Burgess, T., Martin, N., McLeod, A., and Rosen, H. *The Development of Writing Abilities (11–18).* London: Macmillan, 1975.

Burke, J. *The English Teacher's Companion: A Complete Guide to Classroom, Curriculum, and the Profession.* Portsmouth, N.H.: Boynton/Cook, 1999.

Calkins, A. J. *Uncommon Wisdom: Effective Reform Strategies from the 2001 Vanguard Schools.* (Summary profiles). Boston: Mass Insight Education, 2001.

Camp, R. "Portfolio Reflections in Middle and Secondary School Classrooms." In K. B. Yancey (ed.), *Portfolios in the Writing Classroom: An Introduction.* Urbana, Ill.: National Council of Teachers of English, 1992.

Cavanagh, S. "Overhauled SAT Could Shake Up School Curricula." *Education Week,* July 10, 2002, *21*(42), 1, 28. Available on-line: [www.edweek.org/ew/browse_ew_21.htm].

Check, J. "Imaginary Gardens and Real Issues: Improving Language Arts in the Urban Elementary School." *Quarterly of the National Writing Project,* 2000, *22*(1), 2–7, 31–38. Available on-line: [http://nwp.edgateway.net/cs/nwpp/view/nwpr140].

Coles, W. E., Jr. *Composing: Writing as a Self-Creating Process.* Portsmouth, N.H.: Boynton/Cook, 1983.

Coles, W. E., Jr. "Writing Across the Curriculum: Why Bother?" *Rhetoric Society Quarterly,* 1991, *21,* 17–25.

Connors, R. J. *Composition-Rhetoric: Backgrounds, Theory, and Pedagogy.* Pittsburgh, Pa.: University of Pittsburgh Press, 1997.

Cooper, C. R., and Odell, L. (eds.). *Evaluating Writing: The Role of Teachers' Knowledge About Text, Learning, and Culture.* Urbana, Ill.: National Council of Teachers of English, 1999.

Daniels, H., Bizar, M., and Zemelman, S. *Rethinking High School: Best Practice in Teaching, Learning, and Leadership.* Portsmouth, N.H.: Heinemann, 2001.

Darling-Hammond, L. *The Right to Learn: A Blueprint for Creating Schools That Work.* San Francisco: Jossey-Bass, 1997.

Darling-Hammond, L. "Making Relationships Between Standards, Frameworks,

Assessment, Evaluation, Instruction, and Accountability." *Asilomar,* no. 21, Nov. 1999, pp. 1–7.

Delpit, L. *Other People's Children: Cultural Conflict in the Classroom.* New York: New Press, 1995.

Dyson, A. H. *Multiple Worlds of Child Writers: Friends Learning to Write.* New York: Teachers College Press, 1989.

Dyson, A. H. *Social Worlds of Children Learning to Write in an Urban Primary School.* New York: Teachers College Press, 1992.

Dyson, A. H., and Freedman, S. W. "On Teaching Writing: A Review of the Literature." (Occasional paper no. 20). Berkeley, Calif.: National Center for the Study of Writing, 1990.

Dyson, A. H., and Freedman, S. W. *Critical Challenges for Research on Writing and Literacy: 1990–1995.* (Technical report no. 1B). Berkeley, Calif.: National Center for the Study of Writing, 1991.

Elbow, P. *Everyone Can Write: Essays Toward a Hopeful Theory of Writing and Teaching Writing.* New York: Oxford University Press, 2000.

Elley, W. B., Barham, I. H., Lamb, H., and Wyllie, M. *The Role of Grammar in a Secondary School Curriculum.* Wellington: New Zealand Council of Educational Research, 1979.

Elmore, R. F. "Investing in Teacher Learning: Staff Development and Instructional Improvement in Community School District #2, New York City." (Report). New York: National Commission on Teaching and America's Future, 1997.

Elmore, R. F. "Building a New Structure for School Leadership." Paper for Albert Shanker Institute, Washington, D.C., 2000.

Emig, J. *The Composing Processes of Twelfth Graders.* (Research monograph no. 13). Urbana, Ill.: National Council of Teachers of English, 1971.

Emig, J. *The Web of Meaning: Essays on Writing, Teaching, Learning, and Thinking.* Portsmouth, N.H.: Boynton/Cook, 1983.

Flower, L. S., and Hayes, J. R. "A Cognitive Process Theory of Writing." *College Composition and Communication,* 1981, *32*(4), 365–387.

Freedman, S. W., and Daiute, C. "Instructional Methods and Learning in Teaching Writing." In *Subject-Specific Instructional Activities and Methods.* Vol. 8. New York: Elsevier Science, 2001.

Freedman, S. W., Dyson, A. H., Flower, L., and Chafe, W. "Research in Writing: Past, Present, and Future." (Technical report no. 1). Berkeley, Calif.: National Center for the Study of Writing, 1987.

Freedman, S. W., Flower, L., Hull, G., and Hayes, J. R. "Ten Years of Research: Achievements of the National Center for the Study of Writing and Literacy." (Technical report no. 1-C). Berkeley, Calif.: National Center for the Study of Writing, 1995.

Freeman, D. E., and Freeman, Y. S. *Between Worlds: Access to Second Language Acquisition.* Portsmouth, N.H.: Heinemann, 1994.

Fullan, M. *Leading in a Culture of Change.* San Francisco: Jossey-Bass, 2001.

Fulwiler, T. *Teaching with Writing.* Portsmouth, N.H.: Boynton/Cook, 1987.

Fulwiler, T., and Young, A. (eds.). *Language Connections: Writing and Reading Across the Curriculum.* Fort Collins, Colo.: Academic.Writing, 2000. [http://aw.colostate.edu/books/language_connections/]. (Originally published by the National Council of Teachers of English, Urbana, Ill., 1982).

Gavelek, J. P., Raphael, T. E., Biondo, S. M., and Wang, D. "Integrated Literacy Instruction." In M. L. Kamil, P. B. Mosenthal, D. B. Pearson, and R. Barr (eds.), *Handbook of Reading Research.* Vol. 3. Mahwah, N.J.: Erlbaum, 2000.

Graves, D. H. *Balance the Basics: Let Them Write.* New York: Ford Foundation, 1978.

Graves, D. H. *Writing: Teachers and Children at Work.* Portsmouth, N.H.: Heinemann, 1983.

Graves, D. H. *A Researcher Learns to Write.* Portsmouth, N.H.: Heinemann, 1984.

Graves, D. H. *The Energy to Teach.* Portsmouth, N.H.: Heinemann, 2001.

Graves, R. L. (ed.). *Writing, Teaching, Learning: A Sourcebook.* Portsmouth, N.H.: Boynton/Cook, 1999.

Gray, J. *Teachers at the Center: A Memoir of the Early Years of the National Writing Project.* Berkeley, Calif.: National Writing Project, 2000.

Greenwald, E. A., Persky, H. R., Campbell, J. R., and Mazzeo, J. *NAEP 1998 Writing Report Card for the Nation and the States.* (NCES 1999–462). Washington, D.C.: National Center for Education Statistics, Office of Educational Research and Improvement, U.S. Department of Education, 1999.

Harwayne, S. *Going Public: Priorities and Practice at the Manhattan School.* Portsmouth, N.H.: Heinemann, 1999.

Harwayne, S. *Writing Through Childhood: Rethinking Process and Product.* Portsmouth, N.H.: Heinemann, 2001.

Hayes, J. R., and Flower, L. S. "Identifying the Organization of Writing Processes." In L. W. Gregg and E. R. Steinberg (eds.), *Cognitive Process in Writing.* Hillsdale, N.J.: Erlbaum, 1980.

Heath, S. B. *Ways with Words: Language, Life, and Work in Communities and Classrooms.* New York: Cambridge University Press, 1983.

Herman, J. "*Writing to Learn,* by William Zinsser." (Book review). *Quarterly of the National Writing Project,* 1990, *12*(4), 16–19.

Hillocks, G., Jr. *Research on Written Composition.* Urbana, Ill.: National Conference on Research in English, 1986.

Hillocks, G., Jr. *Teaching Writing as Reflective Practice.* New York: Teachers College Press, 1995.

Hillocks, G., Jr. *The Testing Trap.* New York: Teachers College Press, 2002.

Hoff, D. J. "Teaching, Standards, Tests Found Not Aligned." *Education Week,* Oct. 31, 2001, *21*(9), 6. Available on-line: [www.edweek.org/ew/browse_ew_21.htm].

Hull, G., and Schultz, K. (eds.). *School's Out! Bridging Out-of-School Literacies with Classroom Practice.* New York: Teachers College Press, 2002.

International Reading Association and National Council of Teachers of English. *Standards for the Assessment of Reading and Writing.* Urbana, Ill.: National Council of Teachers of English, 1994.

Killion, J. *What Works in the Middle: Results-Based Staff Development.* Oxford, Ohio: National Staff Development Council, 1999.

King, J. A. "Seeing Common Ground: A Parent's Guide to Process Writing Instruction and Assessment." Unpublished manuscript, 1997.

Langer, J. *Beating the Odds: Teaching Middle and High School Students to Read and Write Well.* (CELA report no. 12014). Albany, N.Y.: National Center on English Learning and Achievement, 1999.

Langer, J. *Guidelines for Teaching Middle and High School Students to Read and Write Well: Six Features of Effective Instruction.* Albany, N.Y.: National Center on English Learning and Achievement, 2000.

Langer, J., and Flihan, S. "Writing and Reading Relationships: Constructive Tasks." In R. Indrisano and J. R. Squire (eds.), *Perspectives on Writing: Research, Theory, and Practice.* Newark, Del.: International Reading Association, 2000.

Lewin, T. "College Board Announces an Overhaul for the SAT." *New York Times,* June 28, 2002, p. A12.

Lieberman, A., and McLaughlin, M. W. "Networks for Educational Change: Powerful and Problematic." *Phi Delta Kappan,* May 1992, pp. 673–677.

Lieberman, A., and Wood, D. R. "The National Writing Project." *Educational Leadership,* 2002, *59*(6), 40–43.

Livingston, C. *Teachers as Leaders: Evolving Roles.* Washington, D.C.: National Education Association, 1992.

Manning, T. *Achieving High-Quality Reading and Writing in an Urban Middle School: The Case of Gail Slatko.* (CELA report no. 13001). Albany, N.Y.: National Center on English Learning and Achievement, 2000.

Manzo, K. K. "Schools Stress Writing for the Test." *Education Week,* Dec. 12, 2001, *21*(15), 1, 18. Available on-line: [www.edweek.org/ew/browse_ew_21.htm].

Mass Insight Education and Research Institute. "The Building Blocks Initiative for Standards-Based Reform." Boston: Mass Insight Education, 2001. Available on-line: [www.massinsight.org].

McLaughlin, M. W., and Talbert, J. E. "Contexts That Matter for Teaching and Learning: Strategic Opportunities for Meeting the Nation's Education Goals." (Research report). Stanford, Calif.: Center for Research on the Context of Secondary School Teaching, 1993.

Mencken, K. "When All Meets All." *NABE News,* May–June, 2001, pp. 4–7.

Meyer, L., Orlofsky, G. F., Skinner, R. A., and Spicer, S. "The State of the States." In *Quality Counts 2002.* (Special report). *Education Week,* Jan. 10, 2002, *21*(17), 68–94. Available on-line: [www.edweek.org/sreports/qc02/].

Millman, R. S. "Using Writing to Assess Mathematics Pedagogy and Students' Understanding." In C. R. Cooper and L. Odell (eds.), *Evaluating Writing.* Urbana, Ill.: National Council of Teachers of English, 1999.

Moffett, J., and Wagner, B. J. *Student-Centered Language Arts, K–12.* Portsmouth, N.H.: Boynton/Cook, 1992.

Moll, L. "Literacy Research in Community and Classrooms: A Sociocultural Approach." In R. Beach, J. Green, M. Kamil, and T. Shanahan (eds.), *Multidisciplinary Perspectives on Literacy Research.* Urbana, Ill.: National Council of Teachers of English, 1992.

Murphy, S., and Smith, M. A. "Creating a Climate for Portfolios." In C. R. Cooper and L. Odell (eds.), *Evaluating Writing.* Urbana, Ill.: National Council of Teachers of English, 1999.

National Association of Elementary School Principals. *Leading Learning Communities: NAESP Standards for What Principals Should Know and Be Able to Do.* Alexandria, Va.: National Association of Elementary School Principals, 2001.

National Center for Education Statistics. "Can Students Benefit from Process Writing?" (NCES 96–845). *NAEPfacts,* 1996, *1*(3).

National Council of Teachers of English and International Reading Association. *Standards for the English Language Arts.* Urbana, Ill.: National Council of Teachers of English and International Reading Association, 1996.

National Research Council. *Preventing Reading Difficulties in Young Children.* (C. E. Snow, M. S. Burns, and P. Griffin, eds.). Washington, D.C.: National Academy Press, 1998.

National Writing Project. *Profiles of the National Writing Project: Improving Writing in the Nation's Schools.* Berkeley, Calif.: National Writing Project, 1999.

Neil, S. B. (ed.). *Teaching Writing: Problems and Solutions.* (AASA Critical Issues Report). Arlington, Va.: American Association of School Administrators, 1982.

New Standards Project. *Student Portfolio Handbook: Middle School English Arts Field Trial Version.* Washington, D.C.: National Center on Education and the Economy, and Pittsburgh, Pa.: Learning, Research, and Development Center, University of Pittsburgh, 1994.

Newmann, F. M., Byrk, A. S., and Nagaoka, J. K. *Authentic Intellectual Work and Standardized Tests: Conflict or Coexistence?* Chicago: Consortium on Chicago School Research, 2001.

Nye, J. S., Jr. *Understanding International Conflicts.* (3rd ed.) New York: Addison Wesley Longman, 2000.

Olds, B. M., Leydens, J. A., and Miller, R. L. "A Flexible Model for Assessing WAC Programs." *Journal of Language and Learning Across the Disciplines,* 1999, *3*(2), 123–129. Available on-line: [http://aw.colostate.edu/llad/issues.htm].

Olson, C. B. *Practical Ideas for Teaching Writing as a Process.* (Rev. ed.) 2 vols. Sacramento: California Department of Education, 1997.

Olson, L. "Worries of a Standards 'Backlash' Grow." *Education Week,* Apr. 5, 2000, *19*(30), 1, 12–13. Available on-line: [www.edweek.org/ew/browse_ew_19.htm].

Olson, L. "Finding the Right Mix." In *Quality Counts 2001.* (Special report). *Education Week,* Jan. 11, 2001, *20*(17), 12–20. Available on-line: [www.edweek.org/sreports/qc01/].

Pearson, D. P. "Integrated Language Arts: Sources of Controversy and Seeds of Consensus." In L. M. Morrow, J. K. Smith, and L. C. Wilkinson (eds.), *Integrated Language Arts: Controversy to Consensus.* Boston: Allyn & Bacon, 1994.

Petersen, B. "Motivating Students to Do Quality Work." *Rethinking Schools Online,* 1998, *12*(3), 1, 14–15.

Romano, T. *Clearing the Way: Working with Teenage Writers.* Portsmouth, N.H.: Heinemann, 1987.

Rose, M. *Possible Lives.* New York: Penguin, 1985.

Rose, M. *Lives on the Boundary.* New York: Penguin, 1989.

Rose, M. "The Language of Exclusion: Writing Instruction at the University." *College English,* 1985, *47*(4), 341–359. Reprinted in V. Villanueva, Jr. (ed.), *Cross-Talk in Composition Theory: A Reader.* Urbana, Ill.: National Council of Teachers of English, 1997.

Shaughnessy, M. P. *Errors and Expectations: A Guide for the Teacher of Basic Writing.* New York: Oxford University Press, 1977.

Sheils, M. "Why Johnny Can't Write." *Newsweek,* Dec. 8, 1975, pp. 58–63.

Smith, M. A. "The National Writing Project After 22 Years." *Phi Delta Kappan,* June 1996, pp. 688–692.

Sperling, M., and Freedman, S. W. "Teaching Writing." In V. Richardson (ed.), *Handbook of Research on Teaching.* New York: Macmillan, 2001. (Sponsored by American Educational Research Association).

Storms, B., Gentile, C., Riazantseva, A., and Eidman-Aadahl, E. *Analyzing Classroom Writing Assignments: Lessons Learned from the 1998 Classroom Writing Study.* Princeton, N.J.: Educational Testing Service and National Writing Project, 2000.

Stotsky, S. "Research on Reading/Writing Relationships: A Synthesis and Suggested Directions." *Language Arts,* 1983, *60*(5), 627–642.

Strickland, D. S., Bodino, A., Buchan, K., Jones, K. M., Nelson, A., and Rosen, M. "Teaching Writing in a Time of Reform." *Elementary School Journal,* 2001, *101*(4), 385–397.

Taylor, D., and Dorsey-Gaines, C. *Growing Up Literate: Learning from Inner-City Families.* Portsmouth, N.H.: Heinemann, 1988.

Tierney, R. "Using Expressive Writing to Teach Biology." (Appendix D). In A. Wotring and R. Tierney (eds.), *Two Studies of Writing in High School Science.* Berkeley: Bay Area Writing Project, University of California, 1981.

Tompkins, G. *Literacy for the Twenty-First Century: A Balanced Approach.* (2nd ed.) Upper Saddle River, N.J.: Merrill Education, 2001.

Villanueva, V., Jr. (ed.). *Cross-Talk in Composition Theory: A Reader.* Urbana, Ill.: National Council of Teachers of English, 1997.

White, S. *The NAEP 1998 Reading Report Card: National and State Highlights.* (NCES 1999–479). Washington, D.C.: National Center for Education Statistics, Office of Educational Research and Improvement, U.S. Department of Education, 1999.

Wiggins, G. *Educative Assessment.* San Francisco: Jossey-Bass, 1998.

Winokur, J. (ed.) *Advice to Writers.* New York: Vintage Books, 1999.

Young, A. "The Wonder of Writing Across the Curriculum." *Journal of Language and Learning Across the Disciplines,* 1994, *1*(1), 58–71. Available on-line: [http://aw.colostate.edu/llad/issues.htm].

Zemelman, S., Daniels, H., and Hyde, A. *Best Practice: New Standards for Teaching and Learning in America's Schools.* (2nd ed.) Portsmouth, N.H.: Heinemann, 1998.

INDEX

A

Academy for Educational Development (AED), 46, 49–52, 65–66

Administrators: checklist for, 91–92; role of, in building writing programs, 3, 6, 7, 15–17, 87–105; role of, in teacher professional development, 66, 74, 95–96; strategies for, 88–105; vision and leadership of, 88–89; writing across the curriculum and, 51, 96–105; writing of, 95; writing survey conducted by, 89–93

Alpert, R., 89

Alvarado, A., 58, 61–63

American Association of School Administrators (AASA), 6; Critical Issues Report *(Teaching Writing),* 91–92

Analogies, 40–41

Applebee, A. N., 1–2, 39

Argumentative writing, 23; inquiry-based writing versus, 23–24

Assertion: argument by, 23; unclear support for, 23

Assessment, of writing, 7, 71–85; in classroom, 74–85, 91–92, 93; districtwide or schoolwide survey for, 89–93; elements and techniques of, 77–85; extended writing samples for, 77, 78; impact of, on the classroom, 75–77; instructional purpose of, 76–77, 79; multiple-genre, 77–78, 89; national, results of, 43–46; need for fair and authentic, 15–16; portfolio, 27, 75, 79–81, 83–85; rubric validity in, 78–79; standards alignment with, 15–16, 74, 75–77; state, 74–77; student participation in development of, 82; over time, 79–81; variables of, in states, 75–76; and writing assignment assessment, 91–92, 93

Assignments, writing: assessment of, 91–92, 93; audience communication in, 48; choice in, 48–49; content of, 47; diversity in, 13–14, 16, 41, 49; engagement in, 48–49; ETS/NAEP study of, 46–49; guidelines for, in critical thinking and inquiry strategies, 23–25; guidelines for structuring ideas in, 48; inquiry-based, 23–25, 54–56; in National Writing Project classrooms, 49–51;

research on effective, 46–51; scaffolding in, 24, 48; scope of, 47; writing-as-process strategies for, 23–27

Athabaskan students, 39

Atkinson, R. C., 8

Audience, writing for: in assignments, 48; defining audience in, 26; diversity of, 13–14; importance of, 10, 26; peer evaluation and, 41; reading-writing synergy and, 30–31, 35

Authenticity, 35; of intellectual work, 50

Author's chair (writing strategy), 34

B

Balance the Basics (Graves), 30

Barzun, J., 9–10

Basics, the. *See* Grammar, usage, and punctuation instruction; Product-centered approach

Bay Area Writing Project, 52, 89

Bean, J. C., 24–25, 27

Becoming a Nation of Readers (National Institute of Education), 21–22

Believer-versus-doubter exercises, 24

Berman, S., 87–88, 97–98, 99

Bilingual elementary school, portfolio assessment in, 80–81

Biology, writing in, 52–54

Blau, S., 67

Bonissone, P. R., 101, 103

Boston Writing Project (BWP), 65, 67–69

Brick, M., 98–99

Britton, J., 96

Budget and resources, for professional development, 61, 74

Burke, J., 36–37

Byrk, A. S., 74

C

California, National Writing Project study in, 49–51

California Achievement Tests, 99

California State University, Fresno, 31–32

Calkins, L., 62

Carnegie Foundation for the Advancement of Teaching, 65

CATEnet, 37

CELA. *See* National Research Center on English Language Achievement (CELA)

Center for Research on the Context of Secondary Teaching, Stanford University, 57–58

Center for Restructuring Education, Schools, and Teaching, Columbia University, 60–61

Center for the Improvement of Early Reading Achievement, Michigan State University, 33

Center for the Study of Reading, University of Illinois, 33

Certification requirements, teacher, 5, 59–60

Chafe, W., 30

Chain of unsupported claims, 23, 79

"Changes of state" expository essay, 50

Character development, 50, 55

Check, J., 65, 67–69

Checklist for administrators, 91–92

Chicago Area Writing Project, 80

Choice, in writing assignments, 48–49

City College of New York, 14

Classroom practices: of assessment,

National Institute of Education, 21–22

National Research Center on English Language Achievement (CELA), 1–2, 40, 101

National Research Council, 29, 30, 31

National Staff Developmental Council (NSDC), 61

National writing assessments, 43–46

National Writing Project (NWP), 3, 46; Academy for Educational Development (AED) 2002 report to, 46, 49–52, 65–66; classroom practices of, study of, 49–51; creation of, 2, 4; mission of, 2, 4; overview of, 4–5; professional development model of, 7, 59, 64–69; *Profiles of the National Writing Project*, 66; *Quarterly*, 67–69; sites of, 4; time spent on writing activities in, classrooms, 49; workshops of, 64–69; writing across the curriculum in, classrooms, 51–54; writing strategies used in, classrooms, 49

"National Writing Project, The" (Lieberman and Wood), 68

National-Louis University, 80

Neil, S. B., 91–92

Networks, teacher, 62, 65

"Networks for Educational Change" (Lieberman and McLaughlin), 58

New Jersey, writing standard of, 72

New Standards Project, 82

New York, writing assessment in, 75–76

New York City: Community District 2, 58, 61–63; student portfolio exhibition in, 81; writing across the curriculum in, 88, 100–104

New York State Board of Education, 101

New York Times, 7–8

New Yorker, 9

Newsweek, 2, 36

Nineteenth-century language development model, 20–21

Nolan, K., 64

O

Odell, L., 15

Oklahoma, National Writing Project study in, 49–51

Olson, L., 74

On-demand writing assessment, 75, 76, 79, 83

"Only Thing New Under the Sun, The" (Blau), 67

Opening sentences, 24

Oregon, writing assessment in, 75, 76

"Origins and Structures" writing-across-the-curriculum program, 103–104

P

Pair work, 49, 102

Paradigm shift, 105

Parent involvement, in schoolwide writing programs, 94–95

Pearson, P. D., 29, 30, 33–35, 93, 97

Peer editing: audience and, 41; in classroom vignette, 41; in National Writing Project classrooms, 49; reading-writing synergies and, 34–35

Peer response: in assessment, 82; defined, 27

Penmanship, 1, 39

Pennsylvania, National Writing Project study in, 49–51

Persuasive writing, 23

Petersen, B., 80–81, 82

Phonics, 32, 33

Piaget, J., 22

teaching and, 16; standards and, 71, 74; strategies for systemic, 58; writing's place in, 5–6

School's Out! (Hull and Schultz), 30

Schoolwide writing programs. *See* Writing programs

Schoolwide writing survey, 89–93

Schultz, K., 30

Science: "changes of state" expository essays in, 50, 51; expressive writing in, 52–54, 73; journals, 51. *See also* Writing across the curriculum

Seattle University, 24

Self-assessment, 82

Sentence combining, 27

Shaughnessy, M. P., 14

Short-answer tests, 77

Simmons, W., 74

Single-genre writing assessments, 77–78

Single-test assessment, 15

Site visits, 61, 62

Skill drills, 20, 22, 39

Skills-based approach. *See* Grammar, usage, and punctuation instruction; Product-centered approach

Slatko, G., 40–41

Social studies, writing in, 51–52. *See also* Writing across the curriculum

"Social turn," 28–29

Sociocultural perspectives, 4, 22, 28–29; audience communication and, 30–31; process and skill integration and, 37–39, 40–41. *See also* Diversity, sociocultural

Spelling, phonics and, 33

Staff development. *See* Professional development

Standards, state, 7, 71–75; assessment alignment with, 15–16, 74, 75–77; "the basics" and, 37; examples of, 72; implementation of, 73–75; mathematics standards and, 72–73; national standards and, 72; professional development and, 74; writing across the curriculum and, 97–98. *See also* Assessment

Standards movement, 71–72

Stanford University, Center for Research on the Context of Secondary Teaching, 57–58

State standards. *See* Standards, state

States: assessments in, 74–77; National Writing Project in, 4; teacher competency requirements of, 59–60. *See also* Standards, state

Stookey, H., 53

Story frame, reading-writing synergy and, 34

Story line development, 50, 55

Story writing, 55–56

Structured project approach to learning, 80–81

Structuring of ideas, providing guidelines for, 48

Student Portfolio Handbook (New Standards Project), 82

Student-Centered Language Arts (Wagner and Moffett), 80

Students: diverse abilities and instructional needs of, 13; diverse writing tasks needed by, 13–14, 16; needs of, to improve as writers, 12–14; ongoing challenges of, 14; ownership of writing portfolios, 80, 83, 104; participation of, in assessment development, 82; view that all, can learn writing, 11, 17–18; writing errors of, logic of, 14; writing time requirements of, 12–13, 23, 49

practice in, 6, 12–13, 23, 44, 45, 49; importance of, 1–3, 7–8, 11, 105; to learn, 41, 43–56; mechanics of, 19–22; national assessments of, 43–46; need to expand, curricula, 6; processes of, 21–29, 36–38; product-centered approach in, 19–22; reading and, 4, 7, 29–36; recursive nature of, 10, 25; research on development of, 19–41; as the "silent R," 2, 71; view that all can learn, 11, 17–18. *See also* Teaching, of writing

Writing across the curriculum, 7, 24, 44, 51–54, 96–105; administrators' role in promoting, 96–105; in biology class case study, 52–54; defined, 27; in high school case studies, 52–54, 97–104; in high schools, 51–54, 55, 88, 97–104; history of, 96; movement, 96–97; in National Writing Project classrooms, 51–54; professional development for, 60; resistance to, 97; standards and, 72–73; strategies for, 51–52; thematically arranged interdisciplinary curriculum in, 102–103; as writing-as-process instructional strategy, 27; as writing-to-learn strategy, 51–54, 55

Writing as process. *See* Process, writing as

Writing programs: administrators' role in developing, 3, 6, 7, 15–17, 87–105; checklist for, 91–92; community awareness-building for, 94–95; community involvement in, 93–94; flexibility in, 93–94, 96; long-term planning in, 93–94; preliminary survey for, 89–93; professional development and, 60–61; schoolwide commitment to, 94, 104–105; strategies for creating and sustaining, 88–105; teachers' common expectations in, 15; time frame for developing, 93; vision and leadership of, 88–89; writing across the curriculum and, 96–105

Writing test, in SAT, 7–8

Writing Through Childhood (Harwayne), 63

"*Writing to Learn,* by William Zinsser" (Herman), 55